How not to be a

be a

Soldier

My Antics in the British Army

by
Lorna McCann

Copyright

Dedication

For my daughter, Amy. This book was written to remind you that your mum *did* have a wild side back in the day, so I guess the apple didn't fall that far from the tree. You fill my life with every emotion and I love you dearly.

Contents

Prologue

As the rookie, I was keen to make a good impression with everyone as I didn't want to look like an idiot. I was asked to nip over to the Mechanical Transport (MT) building to collect a long stand for one of the guys in the squadron I'd been assigned to. It sounded like a strange thing but, nevertheless, I was thrilled to have been picked and proudly made my way over. I knocked on Sergeant Babstock's door.

'Enter.'

I popped my head around the door. 'I've come for a long stand, Serg.'

She looked up, smiled, said, 'Come in and just stand there,' and promptly left the office. I'd been standing for about fifteen minutes when one of the troop sergeant majors came in.

'What are you waiting for, Private?'

'A long stand, Sir.'

'Very good, wait there,' and off he went. Within the space of an hour, four more people came into the office and asked the same question. I had no idea that the laughter I could hear in the distance was at my expense.

After the best part of two hours, Sergeant Babstock returned. 'You can go now, Private McCann.' She looked as if she had been crying as her eyes were smarting and her face flushed.

'I haven't got the long stand yet, Serg.'

She started to laugh. 'Oh, believe me, you've had it. Now, off you go.' I left the office really confused and a little annoyed that I was returning empty-handed. It wasn't until I'd wandered halfway across the yard that the penny dropped and I realised just what a "long stand" was. I felt like such an idiot.

I walked into the canteen to a round of applause. Oh, how they laughed. My embarrassment lasted until the next poor rookie eventually came along.

During my first six months, I also asked for striped paint and glass-topped nails. I know, you don't need to say it... I was a fool!

I could only wonder whether, as my parents claimed, the British Army really would be the making of me...

1/ Ups and downs

My childhood was fun, despite my always being in trouble. I'm originally from the north east of England and was raised in a small village called Konnington. My friends and I made our own fun, playing outside from dawn until dusk no matter what the weather. They were happy and exciting times when your mum would open the front door and shout, 'Tea's on the table, time to come in.'

There was no PlayStation, Wii, or Xbox to lure you home and, when you wanted to chat with friends, you went out to play with them. No "virtual" pals on Facebook or Twitter to keep you glued to a computer. Not that you had one of those either.

There was no need for a watch because you either went in when your mum called or when the light started to fade. Of course, you did everything you could to stay out just that little bit longer until she began to shout to you through gritted teeth. By this time, she'd be waiting by the door and, as you ran past her, she'd give you a wallop on your leg for making her repeat herself.

My earliest memory of getting myself in *serious* trouble was at the ripe old age of eight. I'd been playing at a friend's house with my cowboy and Thunderbolt plastic horse. Today's equivalent seems to be Furbacca, the new Star Wars Furby, which comes with an app for your mobile phone so he can be virtually fed, bathed, and played with. How easily pleased we kids were back then.

On my way home in the early evening, I stopped off at the local village shop to look at the penny sweets. I don't know what possessed me, but I picked up a Mars bar and dropped it right into the bag containing the horse and cowboy. The extremely loud "clunk" this made when it fell into the bag must have been deafening, but I couldn't hear anything over the beating of my heart. I bought a penny bubbly and walked home at a fast pace, feeling scared and a little excited knowing I had a Mars bar to eat later, obviously whilst hidden in my wardrobe.

The journey home took less than ten minutes, but that was time enough for the shopkeeper to telephone my mum and inform her of my theft.

Oblivious to anything out of the ordinary, I entered the house to a very sombre-looking mother. She immediately told me she knew I'd been seen stealing and that the police had dropped some forms off for me to sign.

Mum was very upset and said the police may have to take me to jail because I had stolen. I burst into tears and signed my life away on the dotted line. Bearing in mind I was all of eight years old, I didn't possess a signature so had to print my name as best I could. They were probably electricity bills or something, but they looked like police forms to me.

My father was in his usual brown armchair by the fire and didn't once make eye contact with me as he read the newspaper.

'Can't you do something, Mum?' I wailed.

'I pleaded with the policeman not to send you to jail, love, but you *did* steal.'

'Dooooo something, Mum, pleeeeease!' My sobbing increased. Real tears, not my usual crocodile ones.

'Well, he asked if I could think of a suitable punishment instead,' she told me. I know you're laughing at just how ridiculously far-fetched this sounds, but my mother was very convincing and, at the tender age of eight, I assumed I was heading for Hull high security prison. I said I would do *anything* not to go to jail and promised I would never steal again.

My mother told me what she thought my punishment should be. It sounded horrendous, but a much better option than living life on bread and water in jail so I agreed. My father still didn't look at me. I was to do my punishment the following day and it would last for two hours. I went to bed with a heavy heart and no supper. Or Mars bar.

The door to the village shop opened around eleven o'clock the following morning and one of my pals entered. My heart was thumping so fast I couldn't hear anything else. She stopped dead in her tracks and focused her sights behind the counter, wide-eyed. She didn't laugh or say anything; just stared at me with a look of horror. If she'd come in to steal something, that thought was quashed the minute she saw me sitting there, a sign hung around my neck declaring "I am a thief".

To this day, I've never ever contemplated stealing again. Even when I lived on the streets in Germany for a few months with no money and no food, I still couldn't bring myself to steal. Not even to survive. Job well done, Mum!

*****

Over the years, I had my fair share of teenage misbehaviour — smoking, skiving school, and swigging alcohol I shouldn't have been able to buy in clubs I shouldn't have even been in. It was probably a teen thing, but I was going through a funny stage at home and was most definitely not getting along with my mother. She hadn't done anything in particular to make me dislike her. I just didn't like her. It was deemed incredibly uncool to be seen out in public with a parent, so being out with my mother intensified my dislike.

On the day that was to change my life, I had to walk down to the local supermarket in Wytherndale, where we now lived, to assist Mum with the shopping. My only hope was that no-one would notice and she wouldn't do anything out of the ordinary to embarrass me. It was bad enough that she was old. Oh, the fickleness of youth!

I dragged my feet around the store, hoping not to bump into any friends working a Saturday job and, when we left the checkout, I was relieved to be home and dry without incident... or so I thought.

All we had to do was complete the long walk back home and then it would be over. Whilst crossing the road, my mother spotted someone who had a bit of a funny walk. Having a warped sense of humour, she decided to lighten the mood between us by mimicking it. To my absolute horror, she hunched her back and started to drag her left leg behind like Quasimodo. My face coloured immediately and, before I could say anything to bring her to her senses, she stumbled and fell onto her knees in the middle of the road.

I screamed silently. Oh, the shame — here was my mother on a busy Saturday morning, on her knees partway across the road. Her shopping bag fell open and I watched as tomatoes, butter, her purse, and other items scattered everywhere. Her glasses had fallen off and the humiliation was just too much to bear. Thinking as only a selfish teenager can, I grabbed her purse and the butter and started to run. It was one long, straight road home and I ran the length of it at breakneck speed. I was half laughing and half crying and, by the time I got home, I was completely out of breath.

My father was in the kitchen and just stared at me. 'Where's your mum?' I tried to explain she'd fallen, but my words came out garbled and didn't make much sense. He looked furious, grabbed his car keys and left. Around ten minutes later, the car pulled up in the drive and Dad helped Mum out of the passenger seat and into the house. She looked a mess. Her tights were torn, there was dried blood on her knees, one of the lenses of her glasses was cracked, the other was missing completely, and she looked so dishevelled.

Maybe it was nerves, but I started to giggle. My father stared at me furiously. 'Don't you *dare* laugh at your mother. What did you think you were doing, just leaving her in the middle of the road?'

It was a sobering moment and I finally came to the realisation I may have outstayed my welcome at home, something which needed to be rectified. And fast.

The following day, I caught the bus to go to the job centre in Hull. On my way there, I walked past the army recruitment office and noticed a large poster in the window. The picture was of a very handsome soldier in uniform, his finger pointing outwards at me, and the slogan "We pay you to learn to drive" boldly splashed under his photo.

Well, that sounded like an offer I couldn't refuse so in I went like a moth to a flame. I sat down and spoke with the recruitment chap who took me through the finer details of trades and education requirements. He shook my hand and said I would be hearing from them soon and off I went. I decided not to tell anyone about my detour as it was only really an enquiry and there was nothing to report. It's not as if I was really going to join the army... was I?

Two weeks later, I received an official-looking brown envelope in the mail. When I opened it, there were a number of forms that required signatures and I noticed there were two appointment dates booked, one for a medical and one for me to go and sit aptitude and fitness tests. I attended both, but still chose not to announce anything. I passed the tests without problems and all that was left for me to do was pledge my Oath of Allegiance to the Queen and take my consent forms to the recruitment office, signed by my parents as I was under eighteen.

After some thought, I decided now was a good time to inform them of my plans. They were delighted and signed in an instant, without hesitation. No discussion.

That weekend, I was out with friends and told them I'd joined the army. Some were excited for me and some just didn't understand why. As my family were all ex-forces, I suppose it was inevitable I would find my way into the military eventually. Though I suspect my parents' eagerness to sign was partially to get their annoying daughter off their hands.

My Oath of Allegiance signed, soon I had a start date for November 1981. I had officially been recruited by the British Army.

2/ In the army now

After an exciting few weeks' build-up to my departure, heading off to the station in the car with my mum and dad, my suitcase in the boot, was a harrowing experience. I hadn't been away from home before so this was pure adventure for me. Leaving Hull Paragon Station, I had an overwhelming urge to cry, but was already trying to act tough and decided to wait until I was on the train and in a carriage with no-one else. I know my mum would have howled all the way home as we are notoriously a family of criers.

Still, I had made my bed (with hospital corners, just like my mother taught me) and I was going to lie in it no matter what. I mean, what's the worst that could happen? The posters in the recruitment office had made it look like a lot of fun so I was bound to take to it like a duck to water. I'd seen the film *Private Benjamin* featuring Goldie Hawn and had laughed at that, even to the point of imagining myself in her situation.

The train journey down to Guildford was the most exciting train journey I'd ever been on in my life. In fairness, it was almost the only one I'd been on apart from a short train ride to Leeds to see The Specials in concert a few months before. The culture shock of life in the Women's Royal Army Corps (WRAC) was about to hit me like a fast-moving freight train.

Arriving at Guildford was surreal. I stumbled off the train with my suitcase and noticed a large army truck parked out front. I couldn't help but feel that the soldiers who had come to collect us were dressed like women, but looked and sounded like men. Obviously I wasn't going to point that out to any of them.

I gazed around the station where there was a scattering of people just going about their business, oblivious to me or the other soldiers clearly about to start the army with me. I wanted to shout, 'Hey, d'you mind? This is a big moment for me, people, and a little drum roll would be very much appreciated.'

It was some time before I heard a distant voice shouting. 'McCann!' There it was again. I remained glued to the spot and was just wondering what time the next train was back to Hull when a soldier resembling a Russian shot-putter bounded over to me and asked, 'You McCann?'

Had I been offered a million pounds right there to answer that question correctly, I couldn't have done so. I had never in my life seen anyone who looked so intimidating. I was afraid to say yes in case she should have a sinister, ulterior motive for wanting to know my name, but I was afraid to say no lest the others all drove off and left me at the station.

'Hey! You got a name?' she asked in a raised tone.

'McCann,' I quickly mumbled.

'Why didn't you speak up when I shouted your name?'

Bloody hell, I'd only been in the army five minutes and already got off on the wrong foot. I realised I was now gawping and only just managed to reply, 'Sorry.'

'In the back of the truck then, chop chop,' she barked and wandered over to the front of the vehicle. I was one of the last to climb aboard. I silently thanked my mother for insisting I wear jeans and took pity on those girls that had travelled in a skirt, obviously out to make a first impression… suckers! Trust me on this, there is no delicate way of clambering into the back of a truck, no matter what you are wearing. It rates up there with tucking your skirt in the back of your knickers or coughing and farting at the same time. I sat down and looked around. There were seven of us and it was fair to say we all looked equally terrified.

The engine roared into life, the truck shuddered, and off we went. The journey to the camp from the station took around fifteen minutes. I had finally made it to Guildford Barracks. I was unsure if it was too late to change my mind but one thing I knew for sure — I wasn't going to ask my new 'friend' sitting up front. She was only a corporal but, to me, she was pretty scary.

We were ushered in a group to the accommodation block. I had the overwhelming urge to "baa" very loudly and ram my nose up the bum of the person in front of me.

Shown into a room with three other complete strangers, I was left to get on with it. We were faced with a number of options: sit there in silence and say nothing; make idle conversation; or introduce ourselves, break the ice, and start as we meant to go on. Being a nervous talker, I chose the latter and was soon comfortably gossiping with my roommates as if we'd known each other for years.

My room was the "Mc" room. The Mc gang was made up of McDoon, McKinty, McLaughlin, and myself, McCann, and what a fine bunch we were. McDoon was a Scouser, McKinty from Edinburgh, and McLaughlin from somewhere in the south. A nice mixture I thought.

At five foot ten and with chestnut brown hair, my best features were — and still are — my long legs and my eyes, which are green with a blue outer rim. I hated my nose as it had a bump just below the bridge which I thought made it look enormous, but I blended in well with the other girls despite my big-nose paranoia.

McKinty was very shy, plain looking with short dark hair and glasses.

Marginally older than me, McLaughlin was something else. Straight brown hair, a little bit chubby, and with a 55-year-old partner waiting for her at home. At the time that seemed ancient and I remember thinking how strange my roommate was. McDoon was quite fashionable, tall like myself, mousy, shoulder-length hair and quite loud.

Most of the conversation was from McDoon and me. McKinty would be the one to watch as she was most definitely prone to the giggles, the very thing that plagued me all my life. We were shown the toilets which, in this new world, were called the ablutions. Then on to the NAAFI, the army version of a social club, and the cookhouse, which was about as classy as the greasy-spoon I worked in as a teenager. So far, it had felt like a jolly nice day out, although instinct told me that this was but an illusion.

*****

Next morning, all the military staff continued to be very nice to us and it was looking likely that maybe army life would, in fact, turn out to be just like *Private Benjamin*. They would even provide me with a sexy little uniform to wear and tear on my own clothes. How very kind. Tomorrow was the big day when we were to be issued with it and I had already started picturing myself.

The image in my head was along the lines of the main female lead of a '40s' Hollywood movie, maybe Marlene Dietrich, Doris Day, or Rita Heyworth. It included a very sexy pencil skirt, complete with a split up the back, a lovely little fitted jacket, stockings with a seam up the back, and then that dinky little hat — I believe it was called a pork pie hat — that sits on the side of your head. I could just see myself sporting that little number for my return to Wytherndale.

I'm sorry to tell you that my vision of the WRAC uniform was a far cry from the reality. I'd never exactly been a Prada girl but, at seventeen years old, I was now officially dressed like a middle-aged woman. Even my grandma would have turned her nose up at it. How can you get a skirt and jacket so wrong? Not a feminine stitch in their making at all.

The moss green skirt was, quite simply, awful: an A-line shape right down to the knee, reminding me of a child's drawing of a stick lady with a triangle skirt and a leg at either end. This, together with a frumpy matching jacket, a bottle green cravat tie, American tan coloured tights, and flat, black, men's shoes did not make for a happy Lorna. To finish off this hideous ensemble was a dull green beret that only began to take shape when you'd been wearing it for about three years. Until then, it resembled a helicopter landing pad and took a vice-like grip on your forehead and, after ten minutes' wear, left a red rim there too. Great.

But hey, let me not leave out the pièce de résistance… the PT knickers! Yes, they actually issued us with two pairs of the biggest, ugliest, bottle

9

green knickers you could imagine. There wasn't a man alive who would find you remotely attractive whilst you were modelling a pair of those babies.

What we were supposed to do with just two pairs was beyond me. I mean, how humiliating at the age of seventeen to have to do PT in your knickers. I drafted a mental memo to Her Majesty: 'Ma'am, seriously, wake up and get a grip. There are other ways of breaking people. You really don't have to resort to this. The skirt and beret were enough.'

Depression hit me like a brick.

3/ That's the way to do it!

I was lucky enough to have Sergeant Flaggy and Corporal Wright (the latter being the mammoth-sized woman I met at the train station) as my troop leaders. Sergeant Flaggy was short and petite, but could put the fear of God into Freddie Krueger. She had this natural way of looking like she was about to kick your ass if you put a foot wrong. Corporal Wright (Teeny was her nickname) was quite the opposite. Whoever named her Teeny either had bad eyesight, a naughty sense of humour, or a death wish. I still reckon she could have been a successful wrestler and her name should have been Crusher. To be honest, although they were very hard on us, they were also incredibly fair.

Life soon settled into a green haze in which we inhaled and nurtured to the best of our ability. I was a little disappointed that, before I could get the free driving lessons, I had to endure a long list of other tasks like marching, ironing, and the like.

The first time we were shown how to prepare our kit for parade, I thought it was a form of initiation ceremony to see how gullible we new recruits were. After having the "how to iron your socks and large knickers" lesson, it was apparent this was no initiation ceremony, although I was struggling to see the point of ironing underwear. Talk about creating unnecessary work for yourself.

Surprisingly, I did get this task down to a fine art and my ironing shaped up really quickly. I put most of this down to the fact my mum had taught me to iron from the tender age of ten. She had her own drill, starting with tea towels, hankies, and towels, and slowly progressing up to shirts by the time I was around twelve. Anyway, with the aid of Robin Starch, I could iron a crease that would have sliced the morning bread.

Our next task was known as bulling your boots. This is the term used to make the toe of your boots or shoes shine like glass. I'm unsure where the term "bulling" originates — probably short for bullshit. It's most definitely a skill. I've seen people bull their boots for days, only to achieve a matt look finish. On the other hand, I've seen people take half an hour to finish up with the glass effect we all strived for.

The secret is to put a thick layer of polish on the toe of the shoe or boot and then hold a lighter under it for about ten seconds. You then spit on the end of a high quality duster (preferably a jeweller's cloth), add a little more polish to the area of duster that is now damp, and rub lightly in a small circular motion. I think my granddad (the only member of my family to have been in the army, rather than another branch of the forces) must have been shining down on me during my training as I took to bulling like an old hand. I achieved the glass toe effect with the minimum of effort.

Now that we had mastered the art of wearing and cleaning the uniform, we progressed to kit inspection. Once again, I found myself questioning why I was here and whether it was too late for me to go home. The kit inspection really seemed completely unnecessary and just another way to break your spirit. Ha, they probably don't even teach it in today's army due to the human rights law.

Well, for those of us poor bastards who had to endure it, it went as follows: your uniform is required to be folded and laid out in a very distinctive and precise manner on your bed (bed being made correctly, of course, with hospital corners and no creases), which was so methodical it felt laughable. We were each given a photograph of how the bed should look when primed and ready for kit inspection. Once this had been drummed into us and we had spent a few days practising, we foolishly assumed we could put that part of our training to bed. Idiots! How naïve we were to underestimate our trainers…

4/ A rude awakening

I was on a beach with palm trees whispering in the breeze. I could hear the gentle lap of the rippling water caressing the sandy shoreline. I opened my eyes to see Tony Hadley from Spandau Ballet gazing down at me and I was instantly aware we were both naked as the day we were born. He dropped to his knees and ran his finger along my stomach and right down to my belly button, sending my body into spasms. It was romantic yet erotic and I was in seventh heaven.

Until the most horrendous noise dragged me, kicking and screaming, from my sweetest of dreams. 'Please... no, let me finish,' yelled my subconscious desperately. My first conscious thought was that I must be going insane. I could hear bits of metal banging together which couldn't be correct at such an ungodly hour of the morning. Unsure whether I was delighted to be right or horrified to realise that someone was, indeed, banging two bits of metal (mess tins to be precise) together, my eyes widened.

Apparently, this was the alarm for a kit inspection. Just like that. No pre-warning whatsoever.

In a blind panic, my roomies and I scrambled out of bed. Franny McLaughlin fell out and was dangerously close to requiring a crash trolley. We grabbed bits and pieces from our lockers and frantically tried to remember the layout diagram for kit inspection. As I glanced down at my bed, the remnants of my dream and a very naked Tony Hadley were disappearing into the dawn light. My mind was losing the image the more alert I became. It was tragic.

We'd laid out half of our kit before we realised we hadn't made the beds. You have to understand this was four o'clock in the morning and we didn't know our arse from our elbow let alone remember the routine for kit inspection.

Just when it seemed as if things were starting to take shape and a little confidence began to seep through, Sergeant Flaggy and Corporal Wright burst into the room hollering, 'Stand by your beds!' We all stood to attention at the end of our beds and didn't move.

It was during these minutes that I noticed the array of badly tied dressing gowns, slippers, and bed-head hair, and felt mild hysteria rising from the pit of my stomach.

Oh no, not now! I need to explain that the females in our family suffer from a condition called the giggles. It starts somewhere deep in the pit of the gut with the giggles and ends as acute hysteria. It needs nothing in particular to trigger it and, if you don't catch it early, nothing can prevent it taking its course. To catch it in time, you need to develop the skill of training your thoughts to visualise tragedy, death, and destruction.

So there I was, the corners of my mouth slightly upturned in a half smile, my shoulders starting to rise and fall, and my eyes beginning to water. This would really not have been a good time to laugh at anything, so I set my imagination to work fast but, at short notice and being so early in the morning, it was proving very challenging.

I imagined I was at the funeral of a loved one and tried to focus, but it wasn't sufficient. I needed details and beat desperately on the door to my imagination. The image was beginning to take shape and I visualised crying relatives. It was working! The hysteria was heading back down to my gut.

Sergeant Flaggy had reached my bed and bent down to pick up my large, green, and very unsexy army knickers. She started shouting at me and, to my absolute horror, launched them with some force across the room. My mind was reeling as I couldn't remember if they were clean or not. I felt sick at the thought of what she had seen that could have caused her to throw them. I was thinking of apologising for whatever it may have been when, suddenly, the room fell silent. It was as if somebody had pressed a pause button, as all the chaos disappeared and the room went quiet.

I glanced across to see what Corporal Wright was staring at and immediately wished I hadn't. The green PT knickers that had been launched weren't on the floor where they should be; they were stuck to the wall. I could feel the hysteria rising again as this was an opportunity it just wasn't going to miss. How had they stuck to the wall?

The atmosphere changed instantly as both Corporal Wright and Sergeant Flaggy seemed thrown by this. Their bravado disappeared and I believe they may have been on the edge of their own hysteria. They made a sudden excuse to leave and told us to stand easy. The moment the door closed, we could hear laughter.

Without thinking, I walked over to where my PT knickers were dangling and retrieved them. I had to give them a tug but, once they were free, I was able to see a sharp piece of woodchip paper sticking out from the wall, which is what they had caught on. The relief was immediate and I felt the need to point out to the girls, 'They're clean, they're clean. Look… they got caught on this bit of woodchip.'

My dignity was intact and we could hear voices outside the door, which prompted me to race back to my spot by the end of my bed. The corporal and sergeant re-entered the room and I watched in horror as random items were picked up and hurled across it. I don't know which was more intimidating, having your belongings chucked aimlessly or being nose to nose with your sergeant whilst she pointed out (in a very loud voice) your inability to iron and that you were never going to make it through training (which, I have to say, was sounding more and more appealing).

My thoughts reverted to mints. I was finding the close-up coffee breath quite nauseating. It was all I could do not to gag. Maybe the breath was part of the intimidation process.

Thankfully, they left soon after. The usual morning came and went without a mention of the events of the early hours. I wasn't entirely sure whether it had actually happened or whether I'd dreamt the whole thing. I'm sure this is why they pick such an unsociable time of day for a kit inspection.

5/ Life's a gas

There will be a particular event in every woman's life which brings home the realisation that she enjoys the benefits of being treated like a lady. Well, today was my day and it came a week after the kit inspection episode. I really didn't want to be equal to the guys and, if there was a war looming, I wanted to do a job in a nice safe area. The men could do the macho fighting. Women were just not built for that kind of thing.

For anyone in complete disagreement with me, let me explain exactly what it was I was facing that day. I was to complete my gas chamber training. I cannot believe I said that so calmly when what I really thought at the time was so cowardly. *Shit, shit, shit, I can't possibly go into the gas chamber. I get claustrophobic. I get pimples. I'm not feeling very well today. I have nausea. Yes, that's right, nausea like you wouldn't believe.*

Why did we need to be trained in the gas chamber anyway, I wondered? I mean, if in an emergency situation I smelled gas, I would automatically place my gas mask over my head and the problem would be sorted. There really was no need to go to all the trouble of putting this to the test. My imagination was more than adequate, thanks. I got the picture. After an hour of "buts" we were on our way to the chamber.

This was surely to be by far the worst day of my life. I felt like a condemned woman and then a thought struck me... I was under eighteen years of age, so this wasn't actually legal. Was it?!

We arrived at the site and grouped together, hoping for safety in numbers. We looked like scared rabbits caught in car headlights. It's funny but, even though I had been issued with a gas mask and noddy suit (NBC suit — standing for nuclear, biological and chemical), I never in a million years imagined I would need these items. I thought it was just a status thing — if you're in the army you get a gas mask. It was up there with having Meatloaf's *Bat out of Hell* album or one of Chubby Brown's. You didn't have to listen to them, but they were in your collection nevertheless.

My stomach churned and the adrenaline pumped around my body. My only saving grace was the fact I was burning hundreds of calories just with the stress of it all. Every cloud, eh?

We were divided into groups and given a briefing on the morning's tasks. Have you ever not paid attention to the on-board flight safety checks until you hear the pilot announce an emergency landing and you wish you had listened? You realise that, should the plane crash, you'll be the only one on the aircraft having to copy someone else because you don't know what to do. Well, this was a similar scenario. I was so fired up with fear that I hadn't actually taken in any of the instructions.

I donned my noddy suit, checked there was no skin on show, placed the gas mask over my face, felt relief that I could breathe, and waited for my turn. My name was called twice, but I shamelessly ignored it and hoped I would just slip through the net.

Aaarghh, someone tapped me on the shoulder to let me know they were calling my name. Thanks a bunch, mate. I had to force my legs to walk over to the cold, hostile brick building with its one small window. Oh, God, I could see clouds of gas through it and I felt as if I were going to pass out. The hut was made of breeze block and wasn't remotely inviting. I wanted to shout, 'Dead man walking!'

Vivid, happy memories popped into my head from my childhood. I could remember playing on the beach at Wytherndale when we visited my grandparents; spending my youth horse riding every weekend; Christmas at home with the folks, a glass of shandy (made with real beer) with Christmas dinner, sitting round the fire in the evening with turkey leftovers and salad, Mum's homemade pickled onions and Christmas cake. We didn't get many presents, but my parents made it such a magical month, with the run-up and the day itself.

I was almost at the entrance to the brick hut and wondered what it would've been like to have had children, realising I would never have that chance now. You would never believe I failed as a drama student at school because, when the need arose, I was clearly quite the prima donna.

I was beginning to panic. *What if the gas is so thick they can't see if I slump on the floor unconscious and they go back to base thinking I've left the building? No, don't panic, don't panic. You can do this, it's just a bit of gas! I wonder what kind of gas they use. Is there any type other than the one you cook with?*

I tried to reassure myself just to keep walking because, if I stopped, I was in danger of paralysis. My hand reached for the door and I pushed it open. Knocking seemed pointless as you'd only usually knock on a door you wished to go through, and I sure as hell didn't want to enter through this one.

I couldn't see a bloody thing, but a voice immediately piped up from the murky depths, 'Come on in and start walking slowly around the perimeter of the room, breathing normally.'

Breathing normally? Are you kidding me?

The voice again piped up. 'I'm going to light a CS gas pellet, throw it into the middle of the room, and will let you know what you need to do.'

CS gas pellet, what the hell is that? Surely there's already more than enough gas in the room so why do they want to add more? If I can't see anything, how will they know they're throwing the pellet into the middle of the room? What if they throw it too far and the pellet lands on me and the gas gets into my suit and gas mask? Help!

I was now almost at a slow jogging pace as I figured it would be harder to hit a faster moving target. *Oh, God, I can't breathe, I've been gassed. I'm going to die right here in this godforsaken little hut. Life is so unfair.*

Oh, hang on a minute, false alarm. I was just out of breath from running in a gas mask. I started walking again, but my breathing was still very rapid. I tried moving very slowly and, after about ten or twelve paces, realised this wasn't so bad. I had panicked over nothing and I could breathe just fine. I quietly rejoiced.

My happiness was interrupted by the voice of doom. 'I would like you to walk over to the far end of the room and stand with your back against the wall. When you are ready, take a deep breath and remove your gas mask, recite your name, rank, and number and then very slowly walk towards the exit door whilst singing "Jingle Bells".'

My brain froze. I know they seem like very simple instructions, but the situation was surreal and the instructions seemed alien. *Are you flipping serious? Take off my gas mask? Hellooooo! The room is full of deadly gas.*

I tried to work out how deep a breath I should take in order to recite everything and still survive. I was physically frozen to the spot. 'When you are ready, Private,' said the voice.

'OK, OK, don't rush me,' I whispered. I was aware the voice wouldn't be able to hear me due to the hissing sound of the gas pellet, the fact that the room was thick with gas, and I was speaking into a gas mask. I slowly made my way over to the wall and turned around. I took a deep breath and reached up to remove my gas mask. I stopped. *Shit... what's my name? I've forgotten my own name.*

It came back to me. Panic over. I had now run out of breath and needed to take another. Once again, I attempted to remove my mask. *Stop! No, that breath isn't deep enough. I'll run out of air before I've even given my name. Take another.* I became painfully aware I looked like I was hyperventilating.

'Is everything OK, Private?' enquired the voice of doom. Feeling like a fool, I took a huge breath and removed my gas mask. I could feel the gas instantaneously begin to sting my face. Without hesitation, and aware I was a slave to the gas pellet, I shouted out, 'Private McCann, WO470960.' I slowly started to walk over to the door.

'"Jingle Bells", please,' piped up the bloody voice. I began singing it at breakneck speed, sounding like a 45 vinyl record that was set to play at 78. As I neared the exit and was half expecting to be told to do it again, I reached for the handle and opened the door. The beautiful fresh air hit me.

I was alive!

I left the brick hut and closed the door. Someone shouted, 'Run into the wind.' As I started to run, I rubbed my eyes as they were stinging painfully. A massive mistake. The stinging, which was just about bearable, now increased. 'Don't rub your eyes,' yelled the same voice.

For goodness' sake. You might've mentioned that bit first!

The pain was so intense I seriously thought I might be blinded for life. Following a five-minute run head-on into the wind, the stinging began to subside and, as my vision returned, the scene before me was chaotic. There were girls all around me in different states of post gas chamber shock. Some were bent over dry retching, some frantically rubbing their eyes and faces (idiots!), and others just standing, not knowing what to do. Again I reminded myself I should've listened to the briefing when they clearly told you to run into the wind without rubbing your eyes. In fact, I'm pretty sure they would have said, 'Do not, under any circumstances, rub your eyes or face.'

The journey back to camp was grim. Every one of us looked as if we'd been crying all morning as our eyes were red and weepy. Even my pal, Maggie, a lovely Scottish girl who was usually hilarious (and not only after she'd downed a glass or ten of Famous Grouse whisky) was miserable that day.

I always listen to the air stewardess now whenever I fly. I would even go so far as to say I listen so well I could get up and give one of the demonstrations myself.

6/ Best foot forward

Throughout training, we worked towards our passing out parade, which was its grand finale. It doesn't take a vivid imagination to work out that marching is a large part of our tuition so you can see the predicament we had of having the only camel marcher in our squad. Camel marching is built in. You can't fake it for long and, more often than not, you can't cure it either.

When most people march, the left leg moves together with the right arm, and the right leg with the left arm, and so on and so forth. With camel marching, the left leg and left arm move together, and the right leg and right arm move together. It's very comical to watch... until that person is part of your squad.

In a desperate attempt to rectify the problem, we frantically took it in turns, come rain or shine, to drill our pal on the parade square. We were even seen late at night going over and over the art of marching. She would be fine for a spell and then revert back the next day. Training taught me to be tolerant if nothing else.

Over a period of six weeks, we had learned all the various marching steps and commands and had managed to put them into some kind of order. It was amazing how much easier marching looked than it actually was. We were given little counting sequences for each move. Passing out day was slightly different as we were going to be marching with a band and we were very excited by this.

We spent the morning busying ourselves and clucking like hens. The cookhouse had never served up so many full English breakfasts before. We were under strict instructions to have a good hearty breakfast as we would be spending a lot of time on the parade square and the last thing we wanted was to have flakers out there. Did you know that, if you're in squad standing to attention and the person next to you faints, you're not allowed to do a damn thing? You have to let them drop to the concrete. To assist, you need to ask permission and formally step out of attention before you do. It's all very bizarre.

After breakfast, we made our way back to the accommodation block and started to prepare for the big event. Our families were coming and we hadn't seen them for six weeks so emotions were running high. The air was heady with the smell of starch due to the heavy use of irons. Our uniforms were on and we were checking each other like baboons.

We were quite a sight. Our shoes and the peaks of our hats shone like glass. Various girls had sticky tape wrapped tightly around their fingers and were frantically dabbing at random uniforms to remove any bits that may be lurking.

Sergeant Flaggy came in to give us a pep-talk and wish us all well. She told us to take a deep breath and listen carefully to all the commands that were being bellowed out. We told our camel marcher to give it her best and that it didn't matter one iota if she couldn't get it right on the day. It did matter, it mattered a lot, but she didn't need the added pressure.

Nervously, we made our way to the back of the large hangar on the parade ground. All the parents, grandparents, sisters, brothers, and friends were seated in a special viewing area and we were in squad, standing at ease out of sight from our audience. Nerves were fraught and we were secretly praying that our pal would get it right.

Suddenly, Sergeant Flaggy screamed, 'Squa-a-a-d, squa-a-a-d, 'shun!' Our cue to move to the "attention" stance.

It sounded amazing as our feet slammed onto the tarmac in unison to make it sound like one giant foot stamping on the floor. It's a sound you never forget. 'L-e-e-e-ft turn!' she yelled. All that could be heard was the shuffling of us turning left, finished off with one large slam as we stamped our feet into place.

The tension could be felt and everyone seemed to be standing taller than usual. Limbs became as straight as pins and heads were held high. Although you were only allowed to look straight ahead, you could feel the electricity coming off the squad. Suddenly, the band burst into life and, as Sergeant Flaggy hollered out the orders, we followed them to a T.

We marched all around the parade square, going up and down to various different military tunes. On one of the walk-past marches, we received an "eyes right" command and, in the brief instant my head was turned towards the crowd, I managed to spot my mum and dad. Dad was grinning and Mum was crying. I really had to fight back the tears.

It was so clear why we had been drilled again and again. Sergeant Flaggy had drummed into us we had to get it perfect on the day and I could finally see why. If you'd screwed up on this day, it would have been catastrophic. My one regret was that my granddad was unable to be there to see me follow in his footsteps. I had a feeling he was watching me though.

The parade was an extremely emotional event and even our resident camel marcher succeeded in coordinating her arms and legs with the rest of us. I think it remains one of the proudest moments of my life, next to the day my daughter was born.

I had made it through training and was officially a soldier serving in the British Army. I may have only been six weeks older than the day I arrived at Guildford train station, but I had matured immensely and was officially a grown-up. We were dismissed for Christmas break and told to be back by 4th January.

7/ Wheel trouble

Once basic training was complete, we all went our separate ways and moved on to learn our chosen trades, mine being army driver. I clearly didn't think my options through very well prior to making my choice. I would be required to work through the night, drive when exceptionally tired, scrape ice off windscreens on frosty mornings, and wash down my vehicle after a day on a muddy range no matter what size it was. It just didn't sound as glamorous in the cold light of day.

My trade training was to take place at Beconstead, rather handy as Wytherndale was only 25 miles away so I was at least familiar with some of the area.

The man in charge of the MT driver training section was a Welsh sergeant major called Bryn Jones. He had a good set of lungs on him and was one for flirting with the girls, but in a harmless fashion. He was funny and made the day just a little more palatable.

With a new posting came a new set of friends and colleagues although some of the girls from Guildford were also attending driver training so at least we had each other. However, the biggest thrill of all was that we were sharing a camp with boys!

My first night in the NAAFI was a sharp contrast to the one in Guildford. The place was alive with banter and one particular boy I got on very well with stood out from the rest. His name was Scamper.

It was an unspoken rule that, if you started dating someone during your trade training, it was never expected to be a long-term commitment due to the fact you'd more than likely get posted to opposite ends of the country when you finished. He was an average-looking guy, but his personality just bowled me over. He laughed about everything and refused to let life's stresses get to him. With Scamper, the glass was always half full.

One Friday night in January, having had a few too many beers in the NAAFI, Scamper was walking me back to the girl's accommodation block. Whilst taking a shortcut through the MT car park, we stopped for a kiss by a parked Land Rover. Being slightly tipsy, our inhibitions had all but gone and, before we knew it, one thing led to another... like it does. Sober, this would have definitely been a very bad idea, but when you were eighteen and two sheets to the wind... Well, it was fun.

Giggling like a couple of school kids, we fumbled with the Land Rover rope to release the canvas. Attempting to climb into the back when under the influence of alcohol proved to be more difficult that I thought. I had one foot on the tow bar, my head in the canvas, and was hopping about far too drunk to launch myself up and into the back. We were laughing so loud, it was a wonder we weren't heard by the lads on duty. I felt Scamper's hand on my behind giving me a shove with a little too much force, thus propelling me forward into the back of the Land Rover. I was laughing hysterically, waiting for him to climb in with me. His first attempt ended up with him bashing his head on the framework.

'Shit, that hurt!' he laughed. He leapt around on one leg with the other foot on the tow bar and it was just too much to handle. I was cackling like a witch and the more I tried to calm myself, the more I laughed. He attempted another launch and, with a thump, he was on top of me in the back. I was still in the same position as when I landed as I was laughing too hard to make myself more comfortable.

We were still giggling five minutes later when we heard talking outside the Land Rover. The voices sounded like they were about twenty feet away, but were definitely heading towards us. It's amazing how fast you sober up when you think you're about to get caught doing something you shouldn't be. We would be in big trouble if someone found us. We stopped giggling instantly and lay really still. As we listened, the two guys we had heard talking had now turned around and were headed back in the direction of the guardroom.

'Bloody hell, that was close,' Scamper said.

'Do we get out or stay put?'

He turned around to face me with a cheeky grin on his face. 'It'd be a shame to waste the moment now they're gone.'

The adrenaline still pumping through our veins after our close call added to the atmosphere in the back of that vehicle and we began kissing. His hands were all over me and I ripped at his shirt. I gave an almighty tug and it came loose from his jeans. His flesh was warm underneath despite the cold temperature outside and I ran my fingers down his spine. He broke free from the kiss and nibbled my neck and behind my ears. The warmth of his breath made the hairs on my body stand on end and, with the thrill of being dangerously close to being caught, I almost climaxed there and then.

I fumbled with the buttons of his shirt until they were undone and made my way to the zipper on his jeans. Impressively, we managed all this whilst still randomly giggling, but it didn't faze us. His erection made it difficult to undo his jeans and, thanks to my hand and eye coordination not being so sharp due to my alcohol intake, I needed assistance. Once undone, he lifted my jumper over my head and unhooked my bra. His tongue brushed down my stomach to my jeans and he pulled at the button with his teeth.

It didn't seem long before we were completely naked. We were soon writhing around in the back of the Land Rover with me matching his every thrust until I thought I would stop breathing. I don't know if anyone walked past the vehicle or not, but they couldn't have failed to hear the noises emanating from under the canopy if they did. I was holding onto the bars to steady myself and allow myself maximum movement. This sex outside malarkey was a new experience for me. Granted, I didn't have a world of experience with grown-up sex at all, but the bit I had experienced had been a far cry from this.

When we had climaxed we looked at each other and started to giggle again. Suddenly, the voices were back. We instantly fell silent and you could almost smell the fear in the back of that Land Rover. This time was different as we could hear the jingling of keys too. Oh, dear God, we were lying in the back of a military vehicle, virtually naked, and in no position to deny anything should we be found. We were dusty and dishevelled, sweating and, did I mention, we were almost naked?!

I thought whoever was outside would be able to hear my heart beating as, to me, it sounded so loud it was drowning out any other noise. The voices were level with our vehicle when the situation plummeted. Keys were inserted into the driver's door and it opened. This couldn't be happening. Out of all the vehicles in this yard, why had they picked the one we were in? Scamper turned to me and silently mouthed, 'Bloody duty vehicle.' What a vehicle we had chosen to have sex in.

I thought I was going to collapse. My career was going to be over before it had even begun. Shit, I hadn't even passed my driving test yet. How would I explain to my mum and dad that I was being discharged from the army after only ten weeks, and without my driver's licence too? Was I completely stupid? I mean, having sex in the back of an army vehicle… what was I thinking?!

As if by sheer bad luck, the driver wasn't alone. Somebody else climbed into the passenger seat. A nauseating thought hit me like a brick. If there were more than two of them, we needed to brace ourselves for company in the back. The driver and passenger door closed and the two guys talked about a Chinese take-away. The speed with which my blood was racing around my body was making me feel faint and my vision was blurry. Scamper looked like he was going to throw up.

The whole situation was terrible. All we could do was remain still and quiet. The engine fired up and we were off. We could only hope that wherever they were going, they would stop long enough for us to get dressed and get out. I didn't care where we were, I would get back to camp, but at least I would still have the prospect of an army career.

The journey seemed to take forever, but it was probably only five to ten minutes in all. Every corner sent us rolling into the sides of the vehicle and I picked up at least a dozen splinters. We came to a stop and the driver got

27

out. From their conversation on the journey, we discovered that they were, indeed, going to get the duty lads a take-away. My escape plan was dead in the water because the man in the passenger seat decided to stay with the vehicle whilst the driver went in for the food.

I would like to remind you it was January and, up in the north east of the country, the temperature tends to drop incredibly low, so it's safe to say it was freezing, especially given we had no clothes on. Scamper and I shook uncontrollably, but I'm not sure whether this was down to fear, cold, or both.

We waited for the driver to take us back to the safety of the barracks and didn't dare look at each other in case nerves got the better of us and we began to laugh. I prayed I wouldn't break out in one of my fits of nervous giggles.

Thankfully, the passenger didn't look behind him whilst he was waiting. As the driver got back into the vehicle, he handed the bag of food to the passenger and I have no idea how he didn't see us. The delicious smell of food on the return journey made my mouth water and I realised I hadn't eaten that evening. The journey back seemed to take forever. The driver parked the vehicle and we waited anxiously for the men to disappear.

Once they were out of sight and earshot, Scamper and I looked at each other and burst into fits of laughter. We got dressed, checked the coast was clear, and jumped out of the back of the Land Rover. It was an experience that will stay with me forever.

*****

After a couple of hours' driver training in a car, apparently I was ready to move on to a seven-tonne truck. Which idiot decided I was ready for a truck?! A bloody truck — were they mad? I hadn't bargained for this when I chose driving as a preferred career. Just climbing into the cab triggered my vertigo. My driving instructor looked like Lurch from *The Addams Family* so I spent the entire day staring at him. He actually turned out to be a really nice chap who was extremely laid-back.

I soon became one with my truck and enjoyed going out and about, driving in the countryside. Lurch (now my pet name for him) would tell me my destination and would then promptly fall asleep en route. I once circled a roundabout nine times, frustrating the hell out of other drivers in the vicinity, because I didn't know which exit to take and didn't want to wake Lurch. Eventually, I relied on a "technical" expression I had learned known as "ip, dip, dog, shit, you are not it". In my parents' day they chanted "eanie, meanie, minie, mo". Miraculously it worked.

After 29 careful hours of driver training, I had mastered how to start, clean, load, fix my truck, and change the wheels. I passed my driving test with flying colours. The next couple of weeks were spent learning about loads and strapping and passed by in the blink of an eye. Once I'd been equipped with the knowledge of a driver, I was perfectly oiled, prepped, and ready for my first posting.

My training was now complete and I was a fully qualified driver in the British Army.

8/ Space invader

We were herded into a room like sheep to read the listings for our first posting. Mine was Latchmill on Salisbury Plain which I'd never even heard of. My posting wasn't effective immediately so I had a four-week transit period where we were delegated certain tasks to keep us busy. I spent two weeks in the cookhouse peeling potatoes and the next two doing menial tasks. I won't refer to my time as wasted because, to this day, I can peel a potato at breakneck speed.

The camp was enormous and like nothing I'd ever seen before. It was so open and entirely surrounded by 55 thousand acres of plains. Latchmill was the base for the Royal Artillery and it wasn't too far away from Tenworth, a garrison town. The nearest large town for shopping purposes was Salisbury.

My roommates were Nina and Fliss and, as luck would have it, we all got on very well. Nina was the comedian and Fliss was the level-headed one so they were a good balance. My bed space was quite large and it didn't take long to make it reasonably homely. However, there was one thing I couldn't have prepared myself for. My new MT troop corporal was a monster of a woman known as Corporal Vast. I thought the name was someone's idea of a bad joke.

One night, I woke with a start and the strange feeling that someone was watching me. When I turned over and opened my eyes, there was a big, round face leaning over me. The shock made my heart beat so fast I thought I might die there and then. I didn't get a chance to think about my actions, I just went into autopilot. Just as this giant face was hovering above me, I reached out for anything on my bedside cabinet. I had a blown light bulb from the previous night so I grabbed it and clobbered the intruder on the head.

She let out a strange noise, which woke Fliss up, who then started to scream. She didn't even know what she was screaming at, but she set me off and I started to scream too. I've never been able to scream in a high-pitched tone so mine sounded like a male cry coming from my bed space. Nina was up in a shot and started shouting in her Exeter accent, 'Who's there? Who's there?'

Corporal Vast must have wondered what the hell was going on. She jumped up and staggered for the door. As she ran past Nina in the dark, holding her head, she took the full force of Nina's rounders bat on her shoulder. She let out a yelp, but kept running. Eventually, the light came on, the chaos subsided and the giggles set in. Nina joined in and Fliss stopped screaming. She just sat for a moment staring at us before she started laughing as well.

'What the hell just happened?' Fliss asked.

'There was a bloody man in the room,' Nina answered. I decided the best option was to agree with Nina as I didn't fancy my chances grassing on a corporal. I made up a story that he was looking through my drawers and I'd smacked him with a light bulb. The incident was never mentioned by anyone ever again, but Corporal Vast looked shockingly rough the following day. I later discovered she was a lesbian which possibly explained the actions of the previous night.

I've no idea why she was in my room and, in all honesty, it could have been completely innocent. We became quite good friends during our time posted together but, despite that, we never uttered a word about that evening.

9/ Roll call

I rapidly grew to like the MT sergeant, Sergeant Babstock. She was incredibly strict but extremely fair. I didn't always think her fair though. My first morning at the MT yard, as I stood in squad for roll call, I jumped to the conclusion she was a cold-hearted woman. During roll call, you must stand in the "at ease" position. When your surname is called, you stand to attention and shout, 'Sir!' even if the sergeant happens to be female. Similar to a school register being called. Well, except you never had to refer to female teachers as Sir at school.

For the following two weeks, every morning during roll call Sergeant Babstock would call out the surnames until she got to one particular man. 'Coon,' she would shout, and a black guy would stand to attention and shout, 'Sir.' I couldn't believe my ears at just how blatantly rude she was and I was even more baffled why the guy didn't say anything. Being new, I didn't want to rock the boat and speak, but it eventually got the better of me and I did question it. Whoops, his surname was, in fact, Coon. I mean, what were the chances? I went on to meet various other unfortunate military names during my time in the army: Private Sessions, Private Parts, and Seaman Stains (a Navy guy on a course with us) being just a few.

Sergeant Babstock was a large part of my working day. She was a woman of honour and a hugely positive influence on my life. A role model, if you like. If she thought you were in the right about something, she would fight your corner to the death. However, if you were in the wrong, you verbally felt her boot up your arse. The upside was, once she'd torn a strip off you, the issue was forgotten and put to bed. She didn't hold a grudge. She was exactly what someone like me needed as I was opinionated and headstrong.

Dotty was the next person to have a big impact on my life. Five foot seven, with brown hair (short and straight at the sides and curly on top — the '80s were cruel!) and brown eyes, she and I bonded immediately and became inseparable. Of course, it didn't help when Dotty and I formed a tag team. When one of us took a break from the banter and mischief, the other took over. Some of the pranks we got up to should have ended our military career but, for some reason, we were always just lucky enough never to get dishonourably discharged.

Jim Field was the camp Casanova and wooed all the women on a regular basis. If you had a pulse and reproductive organs, you were on his hit list. There was nothing to really dislike about him. He was a complete tart, but very charismatic. He never once denied he was a tart and wore his reputation with pride. Being a physical training instructor (PTI), with handsome dark features that stretched out over all six foot three of him, he had a certain something, that's for sure. Sadly, after about a year of him pursuing me as the new girl, I gave in to his charm and became another notch on his very holey bed post. Life was about learning and Jim sure taught me a few things I couldn't have studied in any school or night class.

Sian was a larger-than-life character in the MT. After being posted with her for nearly two years, I still couldn't fathom her out. She once had a driving detail — an army term for assignment — to Buckingham Palace. By the time we'd eaten breakfast and made it to the troop for morning parade, she'd managed to get a run in her tights not just once but twice (rectified by tying a knot at the top and bottom of them), had ketchup and brown sauce down her white shirt, and still looked hungover (possibly still drunk) from the previous night. We all fell about laughing and couldn't believe she thought she looked presentable enough to go to the Palace. This was what made you love Sian — she really didn't give a flying fig about what people thought of her and I had to admire that. What you saw was exactly what you got, no more and no less.

Tracey, on the other hand, was the opposite and lived, breathed, and ate the army. She was so green it made me want to give her a slap around the back of the head. Her bible was the Queen's Regulations and she refused to even bend a rule, let alone break one. Naturally, she became the butt of most people's jokes. No stories to tell about her I'm afraid as she didn't instigate, or become involved in, anything remotely worth writing about.

There were times I wished I'd taken a leaf out of her book.

10/ They're jammin'

Coming from a small seaside town up north, I hadn't come into contact with many Afro-Caribbean men as there'd only been one black family locally and I didn't really know them. My first introduction to anyone ethnic at all was a down-to-earth private called Wanda, who was mixed race. Her father was black Jamaican and her mother was white. Wanda was from Sheffield and the funniest person you could wish to meet; a walking disaster you couldn't help but warm to. She introduced me to the sound of both lovers rock and reggae music and I adored them instantly.

One weekend, I was excited to be invited up to Sheffield with her. We finished work on the Friday and set off in her Austin Princess for the drive up north. I took over to drive halfway, but every time I used the brakes she shouted at me in her heavy Yorkshire accent, 'Ya wearing me brakes out, use t' gears to slow down.'

When we arrived, she said she had to let her boyfriend, Tony, know she was back, telling me we had to pop into Donkey Man Blues to pick up her door key. I had no idea what Donkey Man Blues was and, with hindsight, I would more than likely have opted out. As it happened, I walked in completely blindsided.

It turned out to be a blues club in a rickety wooden building. When we climbed the stairs to the club and entered, it was pitch black and my eyes took a while to adjust.

'Just wait here and I'll go and find Tony.'

I stood exactly where she left me and didn't move. My eyes started to adjust and I soon felt like a pork chop in a synagogue. The room was dimly lit by little red beads of light in the ceiling, though that didn't prevent me noticing the wall-to-wall, ceiling-to-floor speakers. The air was filled with smoke, and not ordinary cigarette smoke either. I was starting to feel a little light-headed. All around me stood black guys with dreadlocks, chatting or moving to the music. Some of the men simply stared at me and I felt so uncomfortable — not unsafe, but awkward.

It wasn't advised to be in uniform whilst on your own time and especially off camp. I was a very white female — incredibly white, in fact, almost to the point of being transparent — standing in an Afro-Caribbean club, dressed in a military uniform. Alone. When sober, I was a bit of a shrinking violet when it came to people paying me attention and it felt as if every twitch or move I made was being observed. I was scared to look at anyone in case they spoke to me.

The music was loud enough to vibrate through my body and I could feel it buzzing in my teeth. It was alien to me so I couldn't even pretend to sing along, but I loved it. My heart was racing and my palms were sweating. I didn't know how to dance to reggae so just stood there rigidly, cursing Wanda under my breath for leaving me in there for so long on my own.

I'd been standing on the same spot for about ten minutes when a very tall guy approached me. His hair was in dreadlocks and easily reached his bottom. He smiled and asked me for a light. Only too pleased to be able to fit in, I took out my lighter and noticed the cigarette he held to his mouth was *huge*. It was clearly something he'd made himself and was about six inches long. The end he put into his mouth was thin, but the cigarette got progressively fatter towards the other end. I'd never seen anything like it — my first contact with a spliff. He didn't speak, just accepted the light, politely nodded, and returned to his spot on edge of the dance floor.

The music changed and clearly the DJ had a sense of humour as the next song was a very slow reggae song called "She's in the Army Now". Again, I felt out of place and cursed myself for not changing out of uniform before the journey. All in all, Wanda took around 45 minutes to get the key and return. I couldn't get out of there fast enough.

Her family were, thankfully, lovely and we had a brilliant weekend in Sheffield. It was a shame to have to head back to camp, but I soon discovered there was fun a-plenty awaiting me there.

11/ Striptease

There was one particular guy at Latchmill, Shai, who I'd noticed in the disco. He moved like John Travolta and reminded me of Tyrone from *Fame*. His skin was really dark, but so smooth and flawless it was almost like porcelain. He had a really kind nature and the body of a hunky athlete.

After a while, we started dating. My first sexual experience with him came a few weeks into the relationship and was one to be remembered. It was very slow and passionate, and he introduced me to sexual techniques I'd never encountered before. And, no, I'm not going to spill the beans.

As the relationship lengthened, I was too naïve to realise he was an incredible womaniser and would often go out with his friend, Jack, to discos, telling me I could wait in his room for him to return. Inexplicably — pathetically? — I would agree to this and wait for him like an obedient puppy. When you're dazzled by someone, you can't see the wood for the trees. Today, I would laugh at anyone who asked me to wait for them whilst they went out and had a blast chasing other women. I was clueless and actually thought I was "the one" for him. Because he was so attentive around me, I didn't for a second question his motive for wishing to go out without me and, worse still, ask me to wait for him all night.

One Friday evening, he'd arranged to meet me at his place and, when I arrived, he was all dressed up in his *Fame* gear and smelled as if he had bathed in aftershave. He was going out with Jack as a last minute change of plan, but had "kindly" pre-rented me some videos to watch in his absence whilst I waited for him... how very thoughtful. Now, if that didn't reek of a confident man with a gullible girlfriend, then show me another. Lust was clearly a powerful influence for me.

His confidence that I would succumb was clearly well placed as I thanked him, kissed him goodbye, and settled down to watch the first video — *The Evil Dead*. How romantic. Halfway through the movie, I was so terrified I was too scared to get up to turn off the telly. I was glued to the sofa, sweating and shaking and wishing I'd never met him. Even when the film finished and the snowy TV screen appeared, I was still too terrified to get up and change the channel.

I fell asleep sitting upright and had nightmare after nightmare. At three in the morning, Shai returned and woke me by putting his hand under the quilt I had over me to grabbing me. I woke up panic-stricken in the dark, throwing punches wildly, and caught him right on the chin. All hell broke loose and he had to sit on me to restrain me whilst I rained blow after blow on him. I'd turned into the evil living! The relationship dwindled shortly afterwards and I decided to toughen up. From this point forward, I would be no-one's fool.

*****

Groups of lads passed through Latchmill for one type of training course or another and we often got to know them well as they drank in the NAAFI. From one of these courses, I met and started dating a guy called Reno, a really sweet guy. He was so easy to be with and so darned good looking. What a dreamboat. Six foot two with a milky-chocolate complexion, well-trimmed moustache, light hazel eyes, and dimples when he smiled, he had a slim build, but was very well-toned with a washboard stomach.

After an excellent evening of laughter and chatting, we shared a cab back to camp and, when it stopped outside his accommodation block, he invited me in for a coffee. Light-headed with a mixture of sexual tension and a little too much to drink, I agreed. It was all very mature as he opened a bottle of wine and I remember thinking my mother would have been impressed with me drinking wine.

We sat on his bed as there was nowhere else to plonk ourselves, chatted for a while, and sipped our drinks. There was so much electricity between us that the room appeared charged. We paused and a heavy silence fell.

I stood up and walked over to the window to try to get some air from the warm summer breeze coming in. I had taken only a breath when I felt his presence behind me. He reached down, moved my hair to one side, and began to kiss the sides and the back of my neck. I thought my knees would give way. The hairs on my arms and neck stood on end as he trailed small kisses from my neck to my ears, nibbling gently on them. I was completely frozen to the spot. Most of my sexual encounters were either immature fumbles or as a result of too much to drink. This was something I'd never experienced before and it felt a little like a Hollywood movie.

He reached around in front of me to unbutton my blouse and let it fall to the floor. Next were my jeans which left me standing in my underwear. Oh, for goodness' sake, why wasn't there a rule that stipulated that, when going out, you must wear your best undies? Not only were mine lacking on the Victoria's Secret front, they didn't even match. It was official — I was clueless when it came to sexy underwear.

Undeterred, Reno turned me around and removed my bra. Thank goodness it was back in the days when my young, perky breasts remained in the same position when a bra was removed. Today, that very same move could do damage to his toes.

He asked me to take off my pants, which seemed to me like a very odd request. I'd never undressed in front of anyone before and my inhibitions weren't quite vacant enough for this to feel comfortable. I discovered

38

there's no sexy way of removing knickers when under the influence of alcohol.

I hooked my thumbs into the sides whilst trying to be all seductive and slowly tried to work them down my thighs. This became a task and a half as my knickers were firmly planted in the wedgy position. During the '80s, jeans were worn very tightly over normal knickers as thongs were reserved for hookers.

I had managed to slip them down to my knees whilst still holding his gaze. This is where the problem arose as I now needed to look away and bend over to remove them completely, but I suddenly felt sober and foolish. I decided to hook a toe into the side of the knickers and pull them down the rest of the way with my foot. I can offer no explanation as to why I thought this would work well.

I was standing on one leg, with my toe hooked into my knickers, but my foot was stuck and my balance was failing. I began to hop about frantically, trying to free my toe so I could save a little dignity, but it went horribly wrong. Reno was now laughing and I was mortified whilst hopping towards the door. I hit the floor with a thud in what can only be described as a very odd yoga position. I wanted to cry but, when I heard Reno laughing, I saw the funny side and ended up crying with laughter instead.

Sadly, the moment of passion was well and truly gone.

12/ Oh, what an officer's mess

Captain Smartey was the camp adjutant and, to my northern ears, very "hooray Henry". I walked past him in the corridor of the main building one day whilst delivering some paperwork. I saluted him and smiled. The corridor was empty so there was no way for me to escape saluting him. As I walked past, he said, 'Um, Private, pop into my office.' My heart sank. Had I saluted correctly? I did a quick visual check of my uniform and all was as it should be. Oh God, it must have been the smile. Were you not supposed to smile when you saluted? I turned around and followed him into the office where he was waiting at the door to close it behind me.

'Take a seat, Private,' he said sternly. I sat down with a sinking heart. 'Name?' he asked.

'McCann, Sir.'

'Do you know why I have brought you into my office?' His facial expression gave nothing away and he looked a little mad.

'No, Sir, I don't,' I mumbled.

'I have asked you in here because you look like the kind of girl who likes to take risks.' Was it my imagination or did he smirk slightly? My mind raced. I didn't understand what on earth he was talking about. When it came to risks, I was a bit of a coward (bar the incident in the back of the Land Rover). How did he come to that conclusion from a salute and a smile? Was he playing with me? Was this a similar thing to the long stand? What was my reaction supposed to be? Was I supposed to say, 'That's me, Sir.'? It didn't make any sense. I sat looking at him without saying a word.

'Would you say that would be a fair description, McCann?'

'I suppose... '

His smirk turned into a smile and he asked if I had a boyfriend, which seemed a little inappropriate and made me very uncomfortable. I was in his office for ten minutes before he asked if I would like to meet him for dinner that night. Now, that was definitely inappropriate! Even I knew that a private didn't date a captain, it just wasn't done. I was expecting "April Fool" to be shouted suddenly by someone leaping out from a cupboard, even though it wasn't April. The whole scenario just didn't add up.

Was I allowed to say no or was this a double-edged sword where I was in trouble for saying no and in trouble for saying yes? After a very fast deliberation, I decided yes was probably the better option as a no might make him angry and I could end up in even more trouble.

'Come to the side entrance of the mess tonight at eight o'clock,' he said, standing up and heading for the door. 'And come hungry.'

The mess? The officers' accommodation block? I was absolutely bewildered. I saluted him again and left. Here was a captain asking me to dinner in the officers' mess at eight which, I have to say, was a little late for dinner for me. There was a nasty smell about this.

I returned to the MT yard and made my way over to the canteen. Seeing Dotty over in the corner by the food counter, chatting to Jackie, I called her over. I needed to run the situation past a friend as I sure as hell couldn't get my head around it.

'Bloody hell, Lorn, the adjutant?' It turned out that Dotty had as much understanding as I did. 'What're you gonna do?' She fired questions at me sporadically and I couldn't answer any of them. 'Why has he invited you to the mess, but asked you to come in the side door? What're you gonna wear? What's he playing at?' I just gaped vacantly into space. I was starting to get more than a little nervous. Yes, he was a fine-looking man in a devilishly handsome way, but he was a far cry from my type and I didn't fancy him. Oh, bloody hell, what was I going to do?

The day flew by just too quickly for comfort. My friends made their way over to the cookhouse for tea and I made my excuses that I would be dining out that evening, which of course attracted unwanted attention. Everyone wanted to know where I would be going, but I couldn't tell them, no matter how much I fancied the bragging rights.

The officers' mess was a ten-minute walk from the girls' accommodation block and, by the time seven o'clock came around, I was having palpitations. Dotty was trying her best to help, but nothing was able to calm me down. I had tried on all manner of outfits. At least this time the underwear was the most trivial of my worries. That was just too gross for thought. He was over 30 years old which, in my book, made him ancient. I decided on a summer dress, the only item of clothing that made me look remotely sophisticated. It wasn't a look I aspired to.

I set off for the mess building, feeling cheap when I eventually found the side door, yet unsure why. All I had to do was get through dinner then I could leave and that would be that. The door was huge with an enormous brass knocker slap bang in the middle with a doorbell to the side. I wasn't sure what to do, knock or ring. Either way, I had enough savvy to realise it wouldn't be him who answered the door and then what? If I asked for Captain Smartey, I could end up in a colossal amount of trouble. What a dilemma.

As I swapped my weight from one foot to the other and wiped my now sweaty palms on my dress, I decided I was far too young for a heart attack and turned around to make a hasty retreat back to the safety of the girls' accommodation block.

I had just turned when the door opened and Captain Smartey stood in front of me in jeans and a shirt, looking very shifty. 'Where are you going?' he asked, looking a little puzzled.

'Sir, I don't think this is a very good idea. I could get into trouble being in the mess,' I blurted out.

'Nonsense, McCann.'

Oh, great, I was going to have to sit and eat dinner with this bozo and he would refer to me all night by my surname. I just wanted the evening to end and chastised myself for being weak enough to end up here in the first place. He ushered me up a small staircase which was a far cry from the sweeping *Gone with the Wind* style version that sat in the foyer. This was presumably the servants' route. The evening ahead looked grim.

When we finally arrived at what I presumed was his room, I was beginning to freak out. I didn't think we would be eating there. What was the point in that? I wasn't imagining a full introduction around the dining room, but I didn't think I would be eating in his room. Did they even have access to room service?

I walked into a very lavishly decorated room with a four-poster bed, huge windows with expensive looking drapes, and an antique writing bureau. There was a door at the far end of the room which I presumed was the bathroom.

He walked over to the bureau and poured two glasses of red wine. Terrific, I didn't even like red wine, but now didn't seem the time to be choosy. I was going to have to glug it down and pretend. I scanned the room discreetly and my eyes were instantly drawn to the bedside cabinets. In fact, I couldn't take my eyes away from what was on *top* of the bedside cabinets.

On one sat a bowl containing very thinly sliced cucumber, a bowl of strawberries, and a can of squirty cream. The cabinet on the other side had a can of what appeared to be chocolate spray — although I didn't know until I squinted at the label that chocolate even came in spray form — some marshmallows and a set of fluffy handcuffs.

My brain screamed silently. *What the hell are those for?* My blood ran cold as I realised my so-called meal was laid out in front of me. *Is he serious? Have I missed dinner for this? There's no way that's going to fill me up. Just what kind of meal is it anyway?*

I spun around to ask him if it was too late to order anything else, but his soggy wet lips hit mine at breakneck speed, almost smashing my front teeth. There was so much spit, I was in danger of drowning.

It took a few seconds to register what was happening. 'What are you *doing*, Sir?' I shouted. I was still calling him Sir though I didn't know why, given what had just happened.

'C'mon, McCann, let's have some fun and get dirty.'

I could feel myself dry retching. I don't know if it was the image of getting dirty with him, the drool, or the red wine that caused it.

'What are you talking about, Sir, you asked me to dinner,' I shrieked. I realised that grim didn't come close to the way this situation felt. The penny dropped a little late and I turned back to look at the bedside cabinets. Strawberries, cream, spray chocolate! Oh, dear God, this wasn't a meal. These were the tools of his twisted perversions. I lost all sense of decorum when he again came towards me to kiss me with those hideously soggy lips.

'You bloody pervert, don't touch me. I want to leave,' I wailed at him. I no longer cared about rank and I would rather have been caught and charged in this creep's room than face what he had in mind.

'Just relax, you will enjoy it, I promise,' he cajoled, smiling. Did he not hear me? I marched towards the bureau, slammed my glass of awful red wine down on it, turned around and stomped towards the door.

'You can't just walk out of the mess.'

'Watch me.'

He ran over and blocked my path to the door.

'OK…' He hesitated. 'If you want to leave, I'll take you out, but we'll have to be careful no-one sees us.'

I had reached the point where I actually didn't care. He opened the door to check the corridor and turned to wave me out. He was heading for the servants' staircase again. What a creep. I had no intention of leaving the way I had entered so turned in the opposite direction. I marched right down the long hall and found myself at the top of the sweeping staircase that led down into the foyer. I straightened my dress, wiped the remains of the slobber from my face, and walked down the stairs right up to the front door.

I left with my head held high. If I was going to get caught, then I would do it with what little dignity I had left. My blood was racing around my body and I was raging inwardly. I marched down the steps, through the revolving doors and, as soon as I was out of sight of the mess building, I had to lean against a wall as my legs felt as if they were going to give way. I was shaking uncontrollably and didn't know whether I wanted to laugh or cry.

I felt dirty even at the thought of what might have happened. How had I not seen that coming? I wondered if any of the other girls would have had the savvy to see what was happening. Was I really that naïve?

I arrived back at the girls' accommodation block and went straight to Dotty's room. She saw my face and jumped up.

'Christ, girl, you OK?'

I started to babble, the words coming out in a big jumble.

'Shut up, sit down, and drink this.' She handed me a large glass of what turned out to be neat Malibu (aaahhh, the drink of the '80s). I knocked it back in one and, after a deep breath, unfolded the story of the evening to her. Interrupted only by her cries of "dirty bastard" or "cheeky twat", I told her everything. We both sat for a minute staring at the floor. 'You should've taken the marshmallows and shoved 'em up his arse,' she said.

'I should've started a bloody food fight.' We started to giggle and the giggle turned into a fully-fledged laugh. We laughed until our sides hurt.

'Bloody hell, Lorn, I can't believe he did that.' We were still chuckling when someone knocked on her door. 'Who is it?' Dotty asked.

'It's Jackie. Is Lorna here with you?'

'Yeah, come in.' Jackie walked in and looked at me very seriously.

'I've got Captain Smartey on the phone for you in the duty room, Lorna.' Holy shit, why was he phoning the girls' accommodation and announcing himself to the duty girl? Panic rose in me again and I looked at Dotty.

'What am I going to do?' I was almost crying.

'What's going on and why's the adjutant calling you?' asked Jackie, a bemused look on her face.

'Nowt for you to worry about, Jackie, and don't tell anyone he called for her,' Dotty told her with an air of authority. I made my way down to the duty room with Dotty and Jackie in tow and nervously picked up the phone.

'Hello?'

'Hi, it's Captain Smartey. I just wanted to make sure you were OK after tonight and to see if you wanted to meet up another time. I didn't mean to frighten you, but I thought we could spice up the evening. You haven't mentioned this to anyone, have you?' he said calmly.

I had no intention of meeting him for a second time! 'Hello, yes, I told my friend, Sir,' was all that came out of my mouth. No matter what had happened earlier, I still couldn't switch off from the fact he was an officer and, therefore, I should show him some respect. He clearly was undeserving.

'Maybe you'd like to meet up and bring your friend with you,' he replied. He had just apologised for frightening me with the pre-prepared canapés and now he was asking me if I wanted to involve my best friend in his disgusting fantasy.

He was so gross and inappropriate that I flipped. 'You listen to me, you dirty little bastard,' I shouted firmly. 'No, I will not be meeting you again. Nor would I dream of involving my friend. Now, you take my advice and f*** right off and do not call me again,' I ranted through gritted teeth, slamming the receiver down. I felt dizzy and had to sit down.

I looked up and Dotty was staring at me. 'Bloody hell, Lorn, you just told the adjutant to f*** off!'

'Tell me you didn't just tell the adjutant to f*** off! What the hell happened?' asked Jackie.

'You don't want to know,' Dotty and I said together and went back up to her room for more Malibu.

He never bothered me again.

13/ Who shot the captain?

Now this was what I had joined for... a bit of fun! Although the WRAC was a non-combatant corps, we still had to have weapons training which was just *so* cool. The day had arrived and we were going to the firing ranges several miles away. We awoke very excited and couldn't wait to get to the yard. We were marched down to the armoury and issued with a weapon before signing out a sub-machine gun and a box of rounds. We had previously been given instructions and a practical lesson on how to clean, load, and unload our weapons against the clock. By the time we received them, we felt like snipers.

As we boarded the MK (big truck), the morale amongst us was high. On the way, we stopped off for bacon and egg banjos (banjo being a bread roll) and doughnuts. It really was turning out to be a brilliant day. Perhaps what made my view of a good day in the army wasn't quite in keeping with what was expected...

I took a rain check on the banjo, but the doughnuts were a different story. Whenever they appeared, it became competitive and I was the doughnut champ. It had to be sugar doughnuts filled with jam and you had to eat the entire thing without licking your lips. It may sound incredibly easy, but it was far more difficult than you can imagine. Try it and see!

When there's sugar all over your face and jam up your nose, you get an overwhelming urge to lick your lips. This was the day I was to smash my record of two consecutive doughnuts by eating four without licking my lips once. I was a mess but, boy, they tasted good and it was a great source of entertainment for the journey to the ranges. Hey, if you can't laugh at yourself then who can you laugh at?

Anyway, I'm veering off course here. We arrived at the firing range and the excitement was almost too much for us to bear despite our trepidation. There was a smell of cordite in the air and we were champing at the bit to be let loose with a weapon. The place was vast and very impressive, with about five acres of land divided up into different ranges. Although very quiet on the whole, the silence was randomly broken with rapid gun fire in the distance.

Captain Jones (our troop captain) made sure very quickly that we were all in check by bellowing at us and getting us huddled around for a briefing. We were ready.

The targets were at one end of the range and we were at the other. What's the worst that could happen? Ah, you have forgotten that shit happens to me. If anyone could spectacularly screw this up, then it would, of course, be me.

The single-round firing went swimmingly and I did some rather impressive shooting, if I say so myself. At the end of the session, we were told that, if we had any rounds left, we could switch our weapons onto automatic mode and fire at the target, obviously making sure it was clear to shoot. I had clearly not been listening — again — when the instructions were given because I was unaware the gun would handle differently when fired on automatic.

I squeezed the trigger and the strangest thing happened. I seemed to lose control of my body. Instead of firing down the range, I was thrown back by the sheer force of the weapon and lost my bearings. My position shifted and I appeared to have turned slightly to the left, still with my finger on the trigger. Oh boy, was the firing loud.

After what seemed like an eternity, but in reality was probably only a few seconds, it all went deathly quiet. Had I gone deaf? I was shaking a little as the force of the shot had been a hell of a shock. I felt emotional and winded. Out of the silence, I could hear distant swearing and screaming. I turned to see who was making all the noise. I was suddenly very aware that it was directed at me. I didn't understand and everything was jumbled up. One minute I had been an extra in a James Bond movie with the single shot firing and the next minute the captain was screaming and swearing at me.

I was instantly dragged to my feet — the firing had put me on my ass — and frogmarched over to the captain who was bright red in the face and pointing to his boot. I followed his gaze and couldn't see anything. He continued pointing, still swearing and shouting. I looked closer and there it was… the tiniest little nick in the leather of his left combat boot, just above the ankle area.

'You crazy bitch, you shot me! What the hell did I say about firing on automatic?' he screamed in a heavy Scouse accent. 'I distinctly said you were to make sure the area was clear and safe. Are you stupid? Did you not see me?'

He kept repeating himself over and over again. OK, OK, I heard you the first time. He was so angry he was spitting as he screamed at me. Dared I say he was overreacting a tad? Maybe not. I hadn't actually shot him, just his boot and, even then, it was just a nick. I don't know who was more frightened, me or him. I was going to point out I did check and the area I was aiming for had been very clear and safe, however, I hadn't banked on going slightly off course due to the impact of the weapon, but I held my tongue as now was clearly not the time.

The journey back from the firing range was very loud as the girls kept repeating "you crazy bitch, you shot me" followed by howls of laughter.

Luckily for me, by the time we returned to base, he had just about seen the funny side of things and I wasn't placed on a charge. I never did that again!

14/ Guilty as charged

Dotty and I were forever getting up to mischief. It wasn't that we deliberately went out looking for trouble, it just seemed to have a bizarre habit of finding us. That's our excuse anyway. We were frequently in trouble, but never to the point where we were facing a charge... until now. We were both told to report to headquarters.

'Oh shit, Dot, what've we done that can be *this* bad?' I wailed.

'Buggered if I know, Lorn, but it's safe to say we're in deep shit.'

We'd been told to wait outside the commanding officer's (CO's) office. Colonel Thistlethwaite was highly respected, a really fair officer who had come up through the ranks. We sat, nervous as hell, and awaited our fate. My heart beat so hard I thought I saw Dotty tapping her fingers to the beat. The regimental sergeant major (RSM) was a particularly militant bastard and a stickler for rules. Truth be told, he was a complete power freak and carried his cane under his arm, jabbing people randomly just because he could. Today was not turning out to be a good day.

After what seemed like a lifetime, the RSM told us to stand.

'I'm going to march you in, you'll be read the charge, and you'll be asked how you plead,' he barked. 'Once you've pleaded either guilty or not guilty, the CO will award your punishment and you'll be marched out. Is that clear?'

'Yes, Sir,' we both blurted out, terrified. I don't think I've ever been as frightened as I was at that moment. We would be facing several officials in there and it didn't help matters at all that Captain Smartey would be one of them. I really didn't fancy facing him again.

'A-a-a-ten-n-n-tion!' yelled the RSM. *What the hell are you yelling for, we're right here and this is an office block?*

'Ri-i-i-ght turn!'

We did as we were told. Heads were now popping out from behind doors to see what the noise was about. I was as prepared as I could possibly be when the RSM opened the door. I was not going to let the giggles get hold of me. After all, this situation wasn't funny and laughing would only add to it.

'Left, right, left, right, left, right, left, right,' he bellowed. He sounded like a record playing on 78. I could have handled a regular marching pace, but there was no way this side of hell freezing over I could imagine any human being marching that quickly. What the hell did he think he was doing? I had only just managed to calm myself and form a sense of levelheadedness and now he was turning the whole thing into a farce. He marched us in, faster than the speed of sound and, like a pair of broken puppets, we tried to match his pace, but couldn't swing our arms that quickly. We must have looked like a comedy sketch from *The Benny Hill Show*. I watched Dotty virtually jog in with straight arms.

'Halt! Abou-u-u-t turn,' he barked. 'Stand a-a-a-t ease.'

Dotty stopped as instructed and I bashed straight into the back of her as I had quite some momentum going. Benny Hill would've loved it.

We were facing the CO with Captain Smartey directly behind him. It was hard to dismiss images of strawberries and cream from my head. Sergeant Riley was there too as our female representative. It was all very serious and I was struggling to take it in. It was like having an out-of-body experience. I was absolutely terrified with nerves and with nerves come hysteria which was just around the corner. Panic set in.

I don't remember what the CO said. I just remember Dotty's shoulders shuddering. I knew she was on the verge of laughing. I do remember the reason we were summoned in the first place was because we'd decided to disappear to the ladies' toilets in the middle of a very hot day, lie down on the marble floor, and have a little sleep for two hours because it was nice and cool. Some sneaky bugger had come in, not bothered to wake us and reported us to the MT office. Whoops.

It's a scary thing being in front of all those people and nerves sometimes get the better of you. Seeing Dotty's shoulders going was like an open invitation for my hysteria to unleash itself. The tears rolled down my cheeks and I could feel my face contorting, but not a sound came out of us. When I looked up, I saw the strangest sight. The entire group were clearly trying to suppress laughter. Some faces were turned away and others looked as though they were in agony.

Something sharp jabbed me in the back, causing me to jump. It was the RSM behind me with that bloody cane. Ouch. And again. The more he jabbed, the more control I seemed to lose. To the officers in front of me, I must have looked like an out-of-control puppet as I jerked with every poke of the cane. This was just too much for Dotty, and she made a muffled whine. The situation was just unbearable.

The CO suddenly spoke. 'RSM, take these two privates out of my office, get them to pull themselves together and have them back in here in ten minutes.'

'Yes, Sir!'

I didn't know what was going on. Out came the commands again and, once again, we were marching as if on speed. We shuffled out of the office as fast as we could, tears rolling down our cheeks. Once outside, and with the door shut, there was an eruption of laughter from inside the office. I looked at the RSM. He was crimson with fury. I had never seen anybody so livid. He screamed at us to get into the ladies' toilets to sort ourselves out and gave us five minutes flat to get back to him.

We stumbled in, took one look in the mirror, looked at each other and howled with laughter. My jaws and ribs hurt from laughing so hard. Three or four minutes passed before our giggles subsided. We looked at each other, and the realisation of just how much trouble we were in with the RSM finally hit us. Deep, deep breaths and a mental bucket of cold water and we sorted ourselves out and reported back outside the CO's office.

The RSM was still extremely pissed off. We had to go through the whole procedure again, being frogmarched into the office. The CO quickly read out the charge and asked how we pleaded. 'Guilty,' we managed to mumble.

'You will each receive a £30 fine. RSM, get them out of my office.'

He made no eye contact the whole time. I could swear some of the officers still had tears in their eyes from laughing as we escaped.

15/ Graffiti on the car

There weren't many driving details that extremely hot summer so, to keep us all occupied, we were split into pairs and given one Land Rover per pair to strip, prep, and repaint. Yes, I know, all sounds like easy work but, in the blistering heat, we really could have done without being outdoors under the red hot sun with big army boots and a beret on. Very uncomfortable I can tell you. Still, between us, we managed to pass the hours away with a lot of laughter and mucking about.

During the days that followed, whilst we prepped the vehicles ready for painting, Dotty and I were chatting our usual absolute gibberish in the unbearable heat. To be honest, our idea started as small talk and somehow developed into a brainchild of a plan.

We were going to break into the MT yard and spray paint our vehicle with a Chad. For anyone who's a little rusty about street life or too young to remember, a Chad was a piece of artwork — some might say graffiti — comprising the drawing of a wall, with two sets of fingers, a nose, and eyes popping over it. He often appeared with a single curling hair that resembled a question mark and with crossed eyes, and the image always had a slogan across the wall which started with 'Wot, no —?' You then filled in the blank. Sometimes the phrase "Kilroy was here" was spray painted instead.

As we were the ones responsible for prepping and painting the vehicle anyway, we didn't really see the harm and saw it as a morale-boosting exercise. We parked our vehicle for the day in a particular parking bay and waited in our room for darkness to fall. Dotty and I told no-one of our idea and decided on a disguise to enhance our excitement.

After a little deliberation, we went for a Peter Sellers *Pink Panther* kind of look with a false moustache (boot polish), a black hat (beret covered in material from a T-shirt we ripped up), and a long coat (part of our uniform). We looked like the French Resistance. We really did put our hearts into this little escapade. Neither of us had thought of an excuse for said attire should we be stopped by anyone. That was to be the least of our problems.

Armed with a can of white spray paint, we crept out of the accommodation block like ninjas and made our way to the MT yard, giggling all the way. Once there, we climbed over the fence and disappeared amongst the vehicles that were parked up. It was much darker than we had anticipated as the lighting was poor. We had hatched a plan that involved one of us spraying whilst the other would be on lookout. Then we would swap.

The duty battery orderly non-commissioned officer (BONCO) was a guy called Dingo. None of the girls liked him as he was really creepy and always focused on your chest when he talked to you. He also had a bit of a drink problem. As we peered around the back end of a Bedford MK, we spotted him combing his hair (what was left of it anyway) whilst using his reflection in the window. His four cans of Carlsberg Special Brew were safely behind the curtain for consumption later. We made our way over to where we'd parked our vehicle, and Dotty said she would spray the Chad nice and big on the side whilst I kept watch.

Five minutes or so passed. She returned with the spray can, her adrenaline really pumping. I grabbed the can, and Dotty took my post on watch. I made my way over to the Land Rover. It was so dark I could only just make out the Chad. I suddenly realised we hadn't decided on our slogan and ran back to her to discuss. We knew it would have to be funny, and it needed an air of mischief about it. It came to us in a flash… just funny enough to bring to light what a crap night watchman Dingo really was. Mission complete, we snuck out of the yard and back to the block.

The following morning, Dotty and I left the cookhouse with the others and made our way to work. You could actually see the MT yard across the field from the road. As we walked, I noticed something shining brightly from the yard as the morning sun bounced off it. We were all discussing what it could be, but none of us had a clue. It was very peculiar.

Arriving at the MT yard, I sneaked a peek at our Land Rover to check out our handy work. My heart stopped momentarily. How could this be?! Bile rose in my stomach like lava in a volcano, and I thought I might throw up on the spot. There, parked in the exact spot where we had left our vehicle from the evening before, was the V.I.P. Land Rover. It didn't have a canopy and wasn't painted in matt, camouflaged paint. It had a high gloss finish with chrome bumpers and a hard top with windows. There, on the side, in huge white spray paint, was our Chad.

I nudged Dotty and nodded towards the Land Rover. Her face dropped, and she visibly paled. Luckily, we hadn't told anyone of our previous evening's shenanigans, so all we had to do was hold it together and, hopefully, no-one would connect it with us. Ha!

We arrived at work and went into the office to have a little light-hearted banter with the captain, as we always did. It was important to stick to routine. As we desperately tried to remain calm and relaxed, Karen, one of the drivers, came charging into the office shouting in a heavy Devon accent, 'Surrr… Surrr… Someone's vandalised moy waaagon.'

I'm not sure how we would have responded had we not been responsible, but my guess would be not to freeze and remain silent. The boss was onto us. Once Karen's ramblings had sunk in, he spun around and glared at me and Dotty.

'This has you two written all over it. Sit down. Don't bloody move. I'll deal with you in a minute.' With that, he walked out and left us alone in his office.

'Shit, Dot, we've really done it this time,' I whispered.

'Oh, screw it, Lorn, what's done is done.' Although I could clearly see her point, I felt sick and realised I was maybe not as brave as I had assumed. Dotty did look a little pale still, but she remained composed. When the captain returned, he took us to the vehicle and forced us to look at it long and hard. Yep, it was official, we had sprayed the wrong vehicle. Our vehicle had been put in the bays for the evening and, for some unimaginable reason, the V.I.P. Land Rover had been parked in its place.

As I glanced at the vehicle, there, in bold letters was "Wot, no BONCO?" underneath a lovely (if I say so myself) picture of a Chad. How the hell had we managed to spray a vehicle and not notice it was a completely different bloody Land Rover? Was it that our adrenaline had been pumping so much, or was it the few drinks we had consumed prior to the event to give us a little Dutch courage?

The troops were mustered into squad for roll call but, instead of having it straight away, they left us for fifteen minutes to stew. By now, news of the graffiti had spread like a bush fire amongst the troops. The general consensus seemed to be that whoever was responsible should have been plied with free drinks. It seemed so unfair we had to remain silent when we could've had several good nights out on complimentary drinks. The captain didn't have his suspicions confirmed until years later when I had been posted to Kent and came back on a detail for a visit.

16/ Good vibes

I don't know if you remember when Ann Summers home parties were the in thing, long before their shops were deemed acceptable on every high street? One of the girls had organised one in the WRAC accommodation. The build-up was very exciting and we were clucking about our potential new underwear collections, suckers that we were.

The big day arrived and every girl who wasn't on duty was to attend. We had a whip-round, and the duty driver was given money to make a quick dash to Safeway to buy crisps, nuts, sausage rolls, and other snacks for a buffet. The living room was set out with small bowls of nibbles, and we'd bought enough wine to knock out half the army. The lounge area was packed to the rafters, and we waited impatiently, speculating about what we were going to buy.

The moment arrived, and in walked the Ann Summers' rep looking like an air stewardess, dragging a large suitcase behind her. We weren't expecting her to have such an enormous case as we knew the underwear was skimpy. We nudged each other and giggled like schoolkids.

'Right, ladies, I hope you're all up for a little bit of fun this evening.'

We all cheered.

'Bring it on,' I shouted, not for one moment imaging I would later regret those words. The evening started on a high with plenty of wine being passed around and we girls all having a terrific time, sniggering at the peephole bras and crotchless knickers.

The rep spoke over the giggling. 'We're going to have a raffle and there'll be two prizes: first prize and a booby prize for the loser.'

She passed out tickets to everyone and I ended up with number 21. The ticket stubs were folded in half and went into the cup of a size GG bra.

'Right, who's going to pick out the first number?'

Tracey was up in a flash.

'Number ten,' she exclaimed. 'It's the winning ticket!'

Jackie was on her feet in no time, punching the air with excitement, really chuffed to have won a £20 voucher to spend on the evening's wares.

'Right, Jackie, whilst you're up, can you pick a ticket for the booby prize?' the rep asked. 'Come on, Jackie, make it a good one.'

'First time I've rummaged around in someone's bra,' she sniggered as she fumbled around in the cup, yanked out a number, and unfolded it. 'Twenty-one.'

'Yes, yes, yes, that's me!' I cried, punching the air. I jumped up, eager to receive my prize. The host handed me a box, narrow and about four inches long. I was intrigued. I ripped off the paper, opened it up and, to my horror, was faced with a pocket vibrator. The room erupted and the blood rushed to my head so quickly I thought my head would explode.

No amount of alcohol numbed the embarrassing comments that followed for the next five minutes. I was certainly no prude when it came to sex, but I'd never seen a vibrator before, let alone held one and, judging by some of the comments, I wasn't alone. Everyone wanted it to be passed around to hold. How different it is today when you seem to be able to buy a buzzing little friend almost anywhere.

As the laughter died down, there was a yelp from the corner. I looked over to the girl making the noise. She'd inadvertently turned the thing on and dropped it on the floor. Everyone fell silent. All you could hear was a buzzing sound. No-one had thought to switch it on as we passed it around. The room erupted again.

'No need for a boyfriend now, Lorna,' came a shout from the corner.

'I don't know what type of boyfriends you've been dating but, if their dicks have only been four inches long, then you need this more than I do,' I shouted back.

The sex toy eventually made its way back to me and found a place on the floor next to my chair.

'Right, ladies. Are we ready for the fun to begin?' the rep asked.

We all cheered. We thought it already had! Out came the large suitcase she'd dragged in earlier. She unzipped it and brought out a multitude of things that were unrecognisable at first glance. Without sounding like an idiot, everyone knows what a standard vibrator looks like, don't they? Don't they? They're long and plastic with a button on the bottom to switch them on. Well, the stuff that was put on top of the table had never been seen by the likes of us lot at that time. Some had faces, some looked like rabbits, and some had two long bits like a finger and thumb. We spent the evening crying with laughter.

Some of the girls modelled the underwear on top of their Ronhill jogging bottoms and we laughed late into the night. The exhausted rep left the building at around one o'clock in the morning after making a very large amount in commission. I bought some knickers and a joke pair of men's briefs with a face on. Maybe you know the sort? Two round eyes on the front with the iris actually moving around, a nose, and a fluffy moustache. I knew just the person to give them to!

17/ Alarm bells

A group of us had recently become friends with a bunch of guys who were on the same course together. I had hooked up with a lad called Steve. He was incredibly funny and popular amongst his peers. Although he wasn't a particularly handsome chap, he had the best sense of humour and it was this that had attracted me. I decided to play a prank on him.

The men's pants I had bought at the Ann Summers party were just the job. It was a hot, sunny Sunday afternoon and we were all in the NAAFI, having a drink. There must have been around ten of us and we were quite rowdy. At just the right moment, I leaned over and produced a paper bag containing the pants.

'Before you open this, you need to remember that I chose them especially for you. I hope you'll always think of me when you wear them.'

The girls roared with laughter, knowing what was coming. Steve looked a little worried, but bit the bullet and opened the brown paper bag. He pulled out the neat little pants to a warm round of applause and a few choice comments from his mates. They were the topic of conversation for the best part of fifteen minutes, particularly when he put them on over his jeans, jumped onto the table, and gave us a twirl.

It was one of those days where the drink goes down exceptionally well and we could have gone on drinking well into the evening. The bar tender shouted last orders and, after a quick discussion, we decided to get the most sober one of us to drive to the off-licence for a crate of beer so our little party could continue on the grassed area outside the NAAFI.

The driver returned, the beers were passed around, and we made the last of the late afternoon sun. Life was good. We could see a girl running over towards us, yelling her head off.

'There's a bomb scare at the NAAFI. A bomb scare at the NAAFI.' That ruined the mood.

'We're on our way over. Come on, it might blow up.'

These were times when the troubles in Ireland with the IRA were still very raw so a bomb scare on an army base was not out of the ordinary. We were momentarily stunned, but jumped up and gathered the remaining beers.

'Wait for us, we're coming,' I shouted.

'Shit, we were drinking in there just an hour ago,' Dotty added, 'and now there's a flipping bomb.' The tension was high. Corporal Kenco was on duty. He was one of the biggest, leanest men I had ever seen although this wouldn't have helped any of us if it were, indeed, a bomb.

A large crowd had gathered outside the NAAFI and was being kept a good distance away from the building. Why is it that people the world over have to stand and gawp in potentially scary situations instead of legging it? We managed to nudge our way to the front and watched and waited. There was an eerie feeling coming from the crowd. We all knew there could be an almighty boom at any time so we were half on alert to run should the need arise. It seemed like an eternity as we waited... and waited... and waited.

Corporal Kenco emerged from the building. 'Is Private McCann in the crowd?'

I nearly collapsed. I remained silent and rigid. If I didn't speak up they wouldn't see me. I didn't move a muscle and the crowd looked around in search of me. Somewhere behind me, I heard the voice of my allegedly faithful mate, Liz. 'She's here. Why?' I could've throttled her. 'Shit. Sorry, Lorna, were you trying to keep yer head down?'

I moved forward a couple of paces and approached the corporal who was standing at ease, his hands neatly behind his back. The blood rushed to my face and I just knew I was crimson.

'What is it, Corporal?'

'I believe this "package" belongs to you.' He brought his hands forward. From his left hand dangled a pair of PVC smiley-faced men's pants and, from his right hand, hung a brown paper bag. For a split second, the silence was deafening and then, as the situation dawned on the crowd, there was an eruption of laughter and whistles. I had never felt so embarrassed in my life.

The bomb squad tore a strip off me, but at least the issue wasn't taken any further. Someone had seen an unattended brown paper bag on the windowsill when the NAAFI emptied and assumed it to be a suspect package. It's amazing how quickly a situation can snowball, but I learned a valuable lesson that night: always take your pants with you when you leave the NAAFI.

18/ For the first time

Whilst stationed at Latchmill, a troop of US Army soldiers from an airborne unit came over on an exchange from Fort Campbell, Kentucky. A large barbeque and disco were held to mark their arrival, and I was introduced to the sweetest guy. Dave was gentle, fun, and drop-dead gorgeous. He appeared to be the perfect gentleman and the evening was going really well. I'd never even met an American before, let alone a GI.

It was a hot and humid summer evening, causing the drink to have that little bit of an extra effect on me. I was slightly merry before I realised it. I say merry, some might say drunk. I wanted the DJ to play a particular song, but he didn't have the record so I volunteered to run back to my accommodation block to let him borrow my copy. As Dave was such a gentleman, he said he would walk back with me. We stepped outside. A light summer rain was falling, but we didn't care. Chatting away about our families, we slowed our pace when we got level with the sergeants' mess as we were very close to the accommodation block and neither of us wanted this time to end.

The evening was humid and the rain welcome on my bare shoulders. The air was filled with that smell of a forthcoming summer storm. Dave leaned forward to kiss me and I melted. It was so romantic and tender. Somehow, we got lost in the moment and a gentle kiss became a passionate one and oh, wow, he smelled good. We veered off the pathway and ended up around the side of the mess. We couldn't keep our hands off each other. It was exhilarating. His touch ignited my body. I felt dizzy and it wasn't down to the drink.

Somewhere, albeit in a distant part of my brain, a signal was being transmitted to warn me this wasn't a good idea. I was fully aware we were out in the open and there were other people not too far away, but I chose to ignore the signals. I was in too deep and the smell of him was intoxicating. I felt almost drugged by his scent. The bottom line was I had no power to stop myself. That's my excuse and I'm sticking to it.

We hadn't planned for this to happen, but I felt like a surfer faced with a giant wave that was calling. It was almost like it was meant to be. We fell in unison to the ground and, as we writhed around on the grass joined as one, it felt almost animalistic. I had given in to his touch and I really hoped this wouldn't just be for one night, but couldn't help but wonder, at least momentarily, what kind of guy would want to see a girl again if this was the result of their first few hours together. It was absolute madness.

Finally spent, we lay on the grass, breathing heavily and just staring up at the stars. At that very moment in time, I didn't care if the whole of the British Army walked around the side of the building and found us half naked with clothes strewn all around us. Something had awakened in the pit of my stomach and there was an aching in my chest. I thought I might have been in love!

We remained in that position without saying a word for the best part of 30 minutes. After what seemed like an age, he turned to me to whisper, 'You're so beautiful. No-one has ever made me feel like this before.'

What? Cheap? I thought to myself. 'I'd love to see you again,' I replied. 'I'm sorry, I didn't intend for this to happen.'

He leaned up on one elbow and kissed me again. Before I knew it, he was on top of me and making love to me. What seemed like a lifetime later, we dressed and he walked me back to the accommodation. I was on cloud nine. I never did take the record back to the DJ.

The girls were all ears the next morning and I did something I didn't normally do — I remained silent about the evening's events. They had been far too special to share with anyone else. I just wanted to hold onto those feelings and that constant fluttering ache in my chest for as long as I could.

Dave and I saw each other nearly every day for the remainder of his time in the UK and we stayed in touch over the years. To this day, I still hold a special place in my heart for him. I've compared many men to him and wish I had never let him go. I have no idea what he's doing today, but I hope with all my heart he is happy. I really did love that man. In fact, I think a part of me still does… They say everyone has a soulmate and I have a horrible feeling I lost mine.

19/ Pull the pin

I seemed to have a knack of ending up with driving details that no-one else wanted. "Lucky" was not my middle name. However, I was given one particular detail which entailed driving all the way to Otterburn for a week. I didn't even know where Otterburn was so looked it up on a map and discovered it was on the Scottish borders, which filled me with excitement. It was about time I had me an adventure.

My vehicle was a Land Rover and my cargo was to be a sergeant major and a large amount of camera equipment. I woke up in a fantastic mood. I was going on an adventure with a sergeant major and we were going to have such fun. It was summer and the morning was just beautiful. I bounced across to the cookhouse and had a hearty breakfast on my own as it was very early on a Sunday morning. Once I'd finished, I set off to the MT yard to collect my vehicle which had already been pre-loaded with the equipment. All that was left was for me to collect the passenger and we were good to go. I'd pictured him to be a jolly, well-rounded, if not rather handsome, man with a wicked sense of humour.

Arriving at the sergeants' mess, I pulled up outside and waited in the cab of the vehicle as there was no reception desk there and it was long before the existence of mobile phones. As usual, I'd arrived early, but was happy to wait. I'd bought batteries for my boogie box so we could have a good old sing-song on our journey and had made a couple of mixed tapes. I heard the mess door open and, when I looked up from my magazine, my heart sank. A huge gorilla of a man struggled to get his bulk through the door and he limped out, using a cane for support. I'm not sure who I was expecting, but it sure wasn't him.

He mumbled something inaudible when he got into the Land Rover so I just sat there behind the wheel like a lemon. 'Move on,' he added, clearly irritated. It reminded me of my childhood weekends horse riding when you command the horse to move on or walk on. What a miserable sod. I was going to be in for a long week. 'And switch that racket off as well,' he said. Terrific, crappy company and no music. I was going to have to rely on conversation to keep me from nodding off behind the wheel. Either that or die of boredom.

Off we went on what was going to be a very arduous journey. I had set the mile counter to zero when I parked up outside the sergeants' mess and noted we'd travelled exactly 152 miles before he said a word to me. Even then, all he said was, 'I need a piss.' Charming. I pulled over at the next service station and he told me to stay with the vehicle until he got back. He was gone for around twenty minutes. I was bursting to use the toilet but, being the dutiful private, I sat and waited. When he returned, I asked if I could go. 'Well, bloody hurry up!' he cursed. I was beginning to hate this guy. I managed my toilet sprint round trip in four and a half minutes flat.

We continued our journey and, after five hours on the road, I started seeing lay-by signs saying "freshly picked strawberries for sale". I thought it'd be nice to pull over for ten minutes to stretch our legs (although I wasn't sure how much stretching he could do with his gammy leg, poor chap). I suggested we pull in at the next lay-by to get some strawberries and take a short break. 'No, keep driving!' Damn, obviously neither a people nor a strawberry person.

I was starving and longed to crack open the ration pack I'd picked up from the cookhouse that morning, but he didn't give me an opportunity to pull over and eat.

After ten and a half long and gruelling hours on the road with Marcel Marceau, I was instructed to pull into the car park of a very small, starkly white hotel. I was tired, starving, and thoroughly fed up that I was faced with a week with this miserable excuse of a man. This was proving to be the worst detail I'd ever been given and I couldn't see any forthcoming improvement. At the reception, he gave our names and I couldn't wait to get to my room so I could relax and have a snooze. To my horror, I heard him say to the receptionist there was a booking for a twin room under his name. I hadn't stayed in many hotels before, but I assumed a twin room meant we were sharing. I froze and dread swept through me. All respect for his rank had vanished anyway so I blurted, 'Don't we have separate rooms?'

'No, the army doesn't pay for that! We share a twin. You can change in the bathroom.' Unfamiliar with the logistics of room bookings and only just turned nineteen, I wasn't in a position to argue with him. I sank to a new low and dragged the bags up behind me in the direction of our room. Apparently I was also the bell boy.

Later that evening, we sat in the bar after eating dinner. I had a face like a wet weekend in Scarborough and decided to phone Mum as she was always a comfort when the situation felt grim. I told her all about my miserable trip to Otterburn and that I had to share a room with a horrible sergeant major. Her tone changed instantly. She asked for the name of both the hotel and the sergeant major. This conversation wasn't going the way I had planned it. She was supposed to be comforting me and making me feel better, not asking twenty questions about where I was staying and what the sergeant major looked like. Mothers! I cut short the call with the excuse of feeling tired and decided to have an early night.

The following day, we had to go over to Holy Island. Access to this little island is via a causeway that gets covered by water at high tide. With so little driving experience behind me, I really wasn't looking forward to the drive ahead. The road was already beginning to cover with water as we approached. I was absolutely terrified and didn't want to drive across at all. I wondered if this was how a horse felt when faced with a jump that just seemed too large to get over, causing it to refuse the jump. My irritating passenger hopped out of the vehicle, jumped onto the bonnet, and plonked himself down as I hesitated.

'Come on, get bloody going. Time's not on our side,' his grumpy tone snapped me out of my thoughts. I began to shake and was close to tears. I could literally see the tide rising and, although there were marker poles sticking up to mark out the edge of the road, it was difficult to spot the edges clearly. It didn't help he was now partially obscuring my view.

My heart raced in my chest and my eyes glazed over with tears, making it even more difficult to see properly. The poles on each side of the road were about twenty metres apart and were staggered so you could see a pole roughly every ten metres. There is a huge spare wheel sitting on the hood of a military Land Rover, making it impossible to look out of the windscreen in a downwards direction. To add to the danger and already impeded view, this great big fat lump of a man decided to whip out a camera and plonk himself in a sitting position right on top of the spare wheel to film the crossing. It was like a flipping eclipse. I couldn't see the road or the poles and a large chunk of the sea was blocked out by his bulk.

In his infinite wisdom, he shouted that he would guide me across with his voice. Blind panic ripped through me and a strange whimpering noise emerged from my mouth. The tears in my eyes completely washed over this cold-hearted man.

'Bloody hell, girl, get going,' he shouted from his position atop the hood of the Land Rover. I set off in first gear and followed his directions of "left a bit, right a bit". It was like *The Golden Shot* with Bob Monkhouse. I fully expected him to shout, 'Bernie, the bolt!' at any moment. The road wasn't particularly long, but it felt like the longest drive of my life. Several times during the crossing he would scream out, 'Right! Right! Right!' or 'Left! Left! Left!' making me panic and oversteer the vehicle. By the time we got to the other side, I was exhausted and felt physically sick. I got out of the Land Rover and looked back. The road was no longer visible.

I had an overwhelming urge to walk up to him and whack him in the stomach, but held it in check and drove on to our destination on the island. So much for enjoying fresh crab sandwiches and seeing the island's amazing variety of birds like friends envisaged when I mentioned the place.

All I got to do was sit in the darned vehicle and wait for him whenever he wandered off. After a day there, I was so desperate to get away that I didn't bat an eyelid on the return journey although the road was clear of water this time and he was sitting in the Land Rover which did make it much easier. I ate my evening meal and went to bed. This was going to be the longest week of my life.

Next day, we had breakfast and set off for another dull day. Or so I thought. The camera equipment we had brought with us was to be used to film paratroopers in action on a range; some were shooting and others were throwing grenades from behind a wall. It was all very noisy and rather exciting. During the early part of the afternoon, the sergeant in charge of the paras came over to my Land Rover.

'Ever thrown a grenade before?'

Through a nervous laugh, I managed to mumble, 'I've never even seen one, let alone thrown one.'

'Would you like to have a go?' For a split second, words failed me. This was a little too real for me to get my head around if I was honest. I mean — me? Throw a flipping grenade? Really?! After what seemed like an eternity of silence, he decided to answer for me. 'Good, I'll come back for you at sixteen hundred hours.' He disappeared back into the chaos. I sat in the Land Rover trying to process the fact I would be throwing a hand grenade within the hour.

Sure enough, the sergeant returned and escorted me to the wall where the paras had been throwing grenades all morning. He went through a very quick, and far too brief for my liking, drill, explaining in the simplest of terms what I was to do. A very handsome young para was behind the wall and, after hearing the instructions I'd been given, said, 'It's piss easy. You can't go wrong.' This settled my nerves just slightly and I awaited my turn. I think it would've been less nerve-wracking waiting for a bungee jump as the noise was making the whole situation more frightening than it probably was.

'Right, over here,' someone shouted. I shuffled over to the wall, looking petrified, and the sergeant handed me a grenade. It was all very surreal. He acted as if he had only handed me an orange.

'Pull the pin, throw the grenade, and duck behind the wall,' he instructed firmly. Again, I just stood there like a lemon. He must have thought me a simpleton as he said again very slowly, 'Pull... the... pin... throw... the... grenade... and... duck... behind... the... wall.' The handsome para made some room and it was my turn to shine. My hands were trembling so much I almost dropped the grenade.

I looked at the sergeant and he nodded down to the grenade in my hand. I felt a rush of adrenaline and did what any nineteen-year-old, panic-stricken girl would do. I pulled the pin and stood there, the pin in one hand and the grenade in the other. My mind was blank and I couldn't remember the rest of the instructions.

'Throw the bloody grenade! Throw the bloody grenade!' yelled the sergeant. The para was now retreating at a fast pace to safety, which was anywhere away from me apparently. I looked back at the sergeant. His face was crimson and he looked like he was going to explode. 'Throw the bloody grenade!' he screamed again.

My senses returned and I launched the grenade in the direction of the bushes. Before I managed to duck down behind the wall completely, the grenade exploded. The noise was deafening. I was now in a squatting position with my fingers in my ears and, with a very powerful shove, I was pushed onto my bottom by the sergeant.

'What the hell was that about?' He was screaming at me and the handsome para was now on his way back to the wall, presumably feeling it was now safe to re-emerge. 'What? Two instructions too much for you, were they?' the sergeant continued to rant.

I felt like a complete idiot and ran back to the Land Rover where I remained until it was time to leave. With hindsight, I should have screamed back at him, 'Well don't give a young girl a flipping hand grenade and expect her to know what she's doing with it. This is *not* how a WRAC driver normally spends her day.' It was a day to forget, but at least it couldn't get any worse. Or so I thought...

20/ The cavalry arrive

We arrived back at the hotel and my sour-faced sergeant major went to the bar for a drink whilst I returned to the room, had a shower, and then changed. I met him down in the dining room an hour later. If I'd thought the day had already seemed somewhat surreal, what happened next blew me away.

We were at a table for four people and, to my absolute horror, my mum and dad turned up and asked if they could join us. I was absolutely speechless, so fat arse spoke on my behalf. 'And you are?' he asked sarcastically. Oh, God, he had challenged my mother to sarcasm. He was now on a very slippery slope to Loserville. My mother excelled at sarcasm. In fact, she probably invented it.

'We would be Barbara and Chas McCann, this young private's parents.' The sergeant major's face was priceless. A sight I shall never forget. He stammered and stuttered for a while before inviting them to sit with us.

'Do you live up this way?' he asked my father.

'Oh, no! We made the journey deliberately... to see Lorna.' From the tone of his voice, I could tell he was only just about holding his temper. My father was a gentleman and I had never witnessed his temper, but I had heard stories that Dad didn't suffer fools easily. I didn't understand what was going on and dinner was so strained I felt nauseous.

'Fancy a quick game of snooker?' my father asked the now very nervous sergeant major.

'Sure,' he said sheepishly.

Dad and the big lump left the table. It was like a horrible dream. My mother turned to me. 'Have I taught you nothing?' she asked sternly. I wasn't sure how to answer that question because I didn't know what she was getting at.

'What?' was all I managed.

'How can you share a room with him, Lorna? Does that not strike you as odd at all?'

'Well, of course it strikes me as odd, Mum, but I'm a private and he is a sergeant major so I'm not really in a position to argue with him, am I?' I snapped crossly. 'I questioned the twin room and he told me the army doesn't pay for two rooms.'

'He must think you were born yesterday,' she frowned. 'Of course the budget covers two rooms. It's ethically wrong of him to share a room with a young girl like you. I bet he's pocketed the money for one room, blaming the lack of army budget.' How stupid I felt.

My father, meanwhile, had used the game of snooker as an excuse to get this big lump away from the table and outside. Luckily, Dad didn't thump him and I never did find out what was said but, that very same evening, I moved my stuff into a single room. Heaven! No more fat arse snoring and farting through the night. My parents were gone by morning and it was never mentioned again. I really did have the best mother and father a girl could wish for.

En route back at the end of a long week, the conversation was limited all the way. Just as we were entering Aylesbury, there was an almighty crash, shunting my vehicle into the lane for oncoming traffic. Luckily, the road was quiet and there were no cars coming in the opposite direction. 'Shit!' I shouted. I pulled over and got out, feeling extremely shaken.

About five metres back was a side road to the left which now had a Ford Fiesta sticking out of the junction, its bonnet concertinaed. The lady driver couldn't get out as the impact had jammed her door. She wound the window down and said she hadn't seen me as the sun was in her eyes. I looked in the direction she had come from to see the makings of a lovely sunset.

'The bloody sun is behind you,' I grunted. Usually I wouldn't swear at someone the same age as my parents, but I was in shock. Grumpy arse told me to be quiet and took down the insurance details of the driver. I walked over to check the Land Rover and, to my amazement, there was only the smallest indentation and a couple of very small scratches. It really was a solid beast.

Grumpy was more concerned with the camera equipment in the back of the vehicle, but I assured him nothing had even moved. I was sent to trek to the nearest phone box and call 999. Such were the joys of life before the invention of mobile phones.

With the emergency services taking care of the lady in her Fiesta and insurance details exchanged, we continued back. How glad I was to hand back the Land Rover to MT after returning the camera equipment to the store. What an odd week it had been.

21/ It's you and me

Wednesday afternoon was sports afternoon and, if we were lucky, we would go to the gym and be worked on to within an inch of our breathing capacity by some sadistic bastard of a PTI. On the other hand, if we were unlucky, Sergeant Babstock would tell us all to be back at the MT yard for two o'clock in our sports kit because we were going for an eight-mile bash.

I don't know about you, but I would personally prefer the first option, even if the run was only a short distance and would be over with a lot quicker. I hated running with a vengeance and it always seemed to coincide with my sinuses flaring up. It was agony and, when I put my foot on the ground, it felt like my teeth were coming out with every pace. I had asked if I could do circuit training instead as my teeth were sore, but it fell on deaf ears.

It must have been a tougher day than normal this particular Wednesday because we set off on our eight miles of forced marching and jogging over all kinds of terrain. Have you any idea how hard it is to run (whilst already knackered!) over a ploughed field with shin splints and sinusitis? No? Well, let me tell you, it was nigh on impossible. For me anyway.

We were approaching a tank ramp when I lost it completely. As always, I was at the back and Sergeant Babstock was directly behind me, egging me on and giving me the odd nudge forward. Halfway up the ramp, I couldn't hold my temper any longer and out it came.

'For God's sake, stop bloody pushing me. I've told you already, my shins are killing me and I can't run another flipping step. Just piss off and leave me alone!'

I even managed to shock myself with my outburst. Three facts hit me like a bullet: the rest of the girls had stopped running and were staring at us in complete silence; the rank of sergeant meant Babstock was my superior and I could be charged with insubordination; she was a martial arts expert (black belt no less) and could probably kick the shit out of me with her arms tied behind her back.

To my absolute horror, she replied instantly, 'All right, McCann, you want a fight? You got one. No rank, just you and me.' She turned around and bellowed at the rest of the squad, 'You lot, get running back to the yard and wait for me in squad.' The fact she had bellowed this sentence wouldn't have been so worrying if she had said "wait for us." As it was, that distinct "me" was very clear and I had visions of being buried on Salisbury Plain after a slow and painful death at the hands of a mad sergeant with an axe to grind.

Luckily, I saw sense, and the sight of her rolling up her sleeves was enough for me to find a sudden burst of energy, recover from the shin splints, and sprint back to the MT yard. I was so hyped up, I actually overtook the girls and was first back. The incident thankfully wasn't mentioned again which suited me just fine. Even today, I have respect in abundance for that woman.

22/ No such thing as a free lunch

Some time later, Dotty and I decided to learn German and discovered the college in Salisbury was running an evening course for beginners. We joined up and had precisely two lessons. We couldn't get any further than the introduction at the beginning of each class without falling about laughing. It was such a harsh language. After our second and final lesson, we decided to go for a drink in a pub in Salisbury market place.

There were two guys there who were quite nice looking and they came over to talk to us. After chatting for a few minutes, one said, 'We got tickets to see Aswad if you wanna come? They're performin' in Chippenham.'

Just why we agreed to go with these two strangers is beyond reason, but we were live-for-the-moment girls so off we went and climbed into a Ford Cortina with them. Yes, we were idiots. Yet again. The journey to Chippenham was a nightmare. At some point, the driver decided to pop a couple of pills and proceeded to take leave of his senses, driving like a maniac, the car launching into the air and leaving the tarmac over every hump in the road.

Dotty and I did the only thing we could — we held hands, braced ourselves for a head-on collision, and kept our eyes on the road. When we finally got out of the car, it took us all our strength not to drop to our knees and kiss the ground. The relief we felt at still being alive after that journey made it all quite emotional. The drive was over and we had survived. It felt good and we made a mental note that we would take the "safer" option of hitchhiking back.

We went into the concert and they arranged to meet us an hour later by a large pillar a little way from the stage. We should've taken our opportunity and left immediately but, like a couple of fools, we decided to catch some of the concert as we liked Aswad. As we stood by a pillar (the same one they had arranged to meet us at — we were even bigger idiots than you already thought!) they saw us and came over. Damn, they were half an hour early. One of the guys (we didn't even know their names) began to say they were going to be coming back to our place after the gig.

'Sorry,' I shouted back to him over the music. 'You can't come back. Men aren't allowed into our accommodation block.' As soon as I'd said it out loud, it sounded pathetic, even to me. His expression changed and this once relatively good-looking young man now had a sinister and twisted look about him. I realised that tonight had been a catastrophic mistake and the extent of the trouble we were in hit me like a freight train.

My blood ran cold as I felt something sharp press against the flesh of my lower stomach. Instinct forced me to glance down and there, shining up in the disco lights, was a silver blade around three inches long, neatly pressed against my belly. It wasn't pushed hard enough to pierce the skin but, nevertheless, it would leave an indentation.

My survival instinct, which I didn't even know I had, kicked in immediately and I thanked God for the ability to think fast under pressure. I needed to reverse the situation quickly and decided to agree to anything he said. No matter what, I had to make him believe the knife hadn't put me off having sex with him later on (as that was clearly where this was going in his head) so I mustered up a half smile, kissed him (wanting to puke), and said, 'We're not allowed men in the block, but we can sneak you in the back door.' I flashed a dazzling smile straight at him. I just hoped he couldn't smell the fear oozing from me.

Dotty was oblivious to the knife. The minute they were gone, I burst into tears. 'We're leaving! Now!' I told her. She looked puzzled. 'That little shit just held a knife to me when I said they couldn't come back with us.'

'What?!'

'Yeah! Pressed it against my stomach,' I sobbed. 'I had to pretend we'd sneak them in via the back door to keep him sweet.'

'Shit, Lorn, we've gotta get outa here. Come on! Move!'

We made a beeline for the door, frantically looking around to see if they were in view or if we were being watched. Once through the door of the main concert hall, we broke into a running pace towards the exit of the building. Before we reached it, we noticed a stall selling T-shirts. For some reason, we thought that stopping quickly to buy one would be a good idea. I have no explanation for our logic.

T-shirts in hand, we took up the running pace again and didn't stop until we were on the main road heading back towards Salisbury. We found a phone box and called the duty driver. Casey answered the call and, after asking a few of the girls, she came back and announced that no-one was prepared to come out to collect us.

'You really do find out just who your bloody friends are in a crisis,' Dotty swore, thoroughly distressed.

'He held a knife to my stomach, Dot,' I said, in tears again. 'He held a bloody knife to my stomach. Can you believe that?' We walked in silence for about an hour before nerves got the better of me and I started to laugh. We were walking along a road that was pitch black, not a street light or car in sight.

Soon, we noticed headlights behind us in the distance and promptly dived into the bushes at the side of the road. I know this totally defeats the object of hitchhiking, but we were both terrified the approaching car could be the guys and we would be back to square one. This gave us a few problems with the next few cars that passed by as we kept diving out of sight. It was only after a brief discussion that we decided to bite the bullet and stay on the road the next time we heard a vehicle approaching.

The next one was a small van. It slowed alongside us and the driver asked where we were heading. Sheepishly, we said we were going to Salisbury. He wasn't actually going into the city but, after we told him our story, he said he had a daughter about our age and decided to drop us off right next to our vehicle in the car park there, which was incredibly sweet of him. We humbly got out of his van and thanked him again for his kindness.

All the way back to camp, we went over and over how stupid we'd been. What if they'd killed us and dumped us somewhere? No-one would've known where we were because we hadn't told anyone where we were going. They were sobering thoughts.

I thanked my guardian angel and promised to start taking more responsibility. However, I feared that, by now, the angel knew this was my post-situation routine.

23/ Foul play

I had the unfortunate job of being duty driver one stomp night (the army disco) and, after spending an hour over at the NAAFI with half a pint of coke, I returned back to the accommodation block with the sulks. I parked the Land Rover and went straight to bed. The next thing I knew, I was being woken up by Casey in the very early hours of the morning with the news that my Land Rover had been involved in a traffic accident. I may not have been Einstein, but I was fully aware that, whilst I had been fast asleep in my bed, it was highly unlikely my vehicle could have been involved in any mishap.

I stumbled from my warm, cosy bed and wandered over to the window just to humour her, so I was genuinely shocked when I saw my vehicle in full view — down the hill and smashed into the wall of the men's accommodation block. I didn't really have a reaction, but maybe it was just because it was so early in the morning and I was in denial.

Out came the accident report form and my job was to complete it, giving a detailed description of how the accident had happened. I had absolutely no idea what to write as I hadn't the foggiest idea. For once it wasn't anything to do with me. I'd genuinely been sleeping.

Within a week or so, we'd pieced together snippets of conversation and it seemed a small group of lads had decided (whilst drunk, of course) to move my vehicle to another parking space for a bit of a giggle. How could I moan about that, given all the pranks I'd played? They'd taken off the handbrake and started to roll the vehicle down the hill, without taking into account the fact the steering lock would come on when they tried to go around the big wheelie bin.

Nor had they factored in the laws of gravity as the vehicle followed the natural descent of the enormously steep hill. As it gained momentum, they realised they'd lost control and all of them scarpered, leaving the vehicle to its own devices, which just happened to be aiming for the men's accommodation block.

Karma crept in though as the Land Rover hit the exact same piece of the building where one of the lads had parked his motorcycle (which was his pride and joy), expertly crushing it with no mercy. The outcome was foul play but, for some months after, I'm pretty sure some people thought I was involved.

24/ Pimp your ride

Many courses of soldiers came and went and, on one of them, was a chap called Earl. He was a nice enough character and Dotty and I soon became friendly with him. He was a Rastafarian, but without the dreadlocks, and was so laid-back that sometimes you wanted to check for a pulse. The fact he drove a BMW 7 Series had nothing to do with our friendship. Really!

Anyway, Earl was more like an older brother to us. He would take us out shopping in his fantastic car and generally look out for us. After a few weeks, he announced one day at breakfast that he was going to Bavaria for a few days with the army and asked if we would look after the car. We agreed to keep an eye on it and take it for a little drive each day around the camp. No hardship for us at all.

Sometimes Dotty and I would just sit in it for the sake of it, although not for too long as there was a funny smell inside. As for driving it anywhere, that was a luxury we just couldn't afford. Have you any idea how much it cost to put petrol into a BMW 7 Series? Too much for us, that's for sure. Happy in the knowledge we could just pose in it every now and again, we were content. That is, until we had "the calling" one day whilst at work.

We were told to report to Major Hamilton who was one hell of a scary bitch. Panic set in and we couldn't think of anything we had done that was bad enough to warrant being summoned. If you haven't been in the military, then I should tell you that soldiers have been called in front of a major in error occasionally. We hoped this was the case.

On the journey from the MT yard to the HQ offices, we were both very subdued. Once there, we were kept waiting for fifteen minutes. The only thing that stopped us from running was the fact that, every time an officer walked down the corridor, we had to stand up and salute. In that short fifteen minutes we were up and down like a tart's drawers.

Sergeant Riley came out of the office to escort us in and we were partly relieved to see her as she was so nice. I couldn't believe we were here again. Dotty and I were sent in separately to see Major Hamilton. I was first and stood in front of her desk, frozen with fear at the sight of not just her, but the military police alongside her. Two plainclothes women from the Special Investigation Branch (SIB) were introduced to me. Their names were irrelevant to me at the time, but who they represented was very relevant.

This was clearly not going to be a coffee-and-a-custard-cream kind of meeting. There wasn't even any small talk. Just straight to the point, from the mouth of one of the SIB women. 'So, tell us how well you know Tyrone Smart?'

Ha, it was all obviously a huge misunderstanding. They had the wrong people because I'd never heard of him. You could probably just about smell my relief.

'Who?'

'Don't be smart. Let me rephrase the question. How long have you been working for Tyrone Smart?'

I didn't get a chance to answer the barrage of questions that followed for the next five minutes. I just kept telling them I didn't have a clue who they were talking about and I wasn't working for anyone. Although terrified, and with no idea who this Tyrone Smart was, I couldn't have been more surprised when papers were pushed in front of me with the announcement that these were my discharge papers. I thought I was going to faint, such was the rush of blood to my head.

I don't know if it was the genuinely confused look on my face that made them believe me or not, but Sergeant Riley spoke up and said she was sure I was telling the truth.

I was sent out of the office and Dotty was escorted in. She was there for 90 minutes. She was white as a sheet when she came out. We were left outside the office feeling confused and scared whilst they deliberated our situation. So scared were we that, for once, we didn't say a word.

Twenty minutes later, we were called back in and Major Hamilton filled us in with the details of the investigation. It turned out that Tyrone Smart was the very same person as Earl, and it also turned out he wasn't quite the person Dotty and I thought he was. He had been trafficking drugs from Amsterdam on a regular basis and was also a pimp. A pimp!

He had been under surveillance for some time and was captured on the Holland border with drugs. Bavaria my arse! To top it all, the lovely BMW Dotty and I were so kindly looking after and sitting in on a regular basis was laden with weed. That explained the funny smell.

That was the closest I had ever come to a dishonourable discharge, and the last time I ever looked after anyone's car.

25/ Beyond bravery

At Latchmill, we had a troop of Pioneer Corps. They wore a khaki coloured beret and had a reputation for allegedly not being the brightest lights on the tree, hence their nickname — Planks. Looking back, a soldier is a soldier, regardless of the regiment and shouldn't be looked down upon. Anyway, I collected my detail this particular morning and I was to pick up twenty men in a Bedford TK truck.

When I arrived at their unit, nineteen climbed in the back and one got in the cab with me. I had never seen such a scruffy bunch of soldiers in all my life. Their clothes were creased and they weren't even wearing regulation uniform. Their hair was way below the collar (the RSM would have a field day with them for that) and they just looked like a bunch of slovenly fools.

My job was to drive them out onto Salisbury Plain, wait for the day, and return back to unit at the end of the day. On the outward journey, I thought I would make a little small talk with the chap sharing the cab. My first mistake was to ask, 'How long have you been with the Pioneer Corps?' closely followed by, 'Are you Territorial Army?'

If looks could've killed, I wouldn't be telling this story today. Receiving only a grunt and a filthy look in reply, I decided he was clearly not the talkative type and I'd be better off keeping my conversation to myself. Not only were they scruffy bastards, but rude as well.

Arriving at the plain, I noticed a Hercules aircraft and two spotter planes flying overhead. They appeared to be circling. I saw one of the guys from my MT unit and made my way over to him for a chat and a smoke. He had driven the sergeant major in charge.

'Pioneer are bloody miserable bastards, aren't they? Got their heads stuck up their own arses,' I muttered. Bob started to laugh.

'Did you refer to them as Pioneers?'

'Yeah, I tried to make conversation with the one in the passenger seat, asked him how long he'd been with the Pioneers and if they were TA.'

He grinned. 'You will *not* be popular with this lot today then.'

'Why?'

'They're bloody SAS! No wonder he didn't talk to you. You just insulted him.'

What a fool. How was I going to face them on the return journey? 'Why am I driving the SAS out onto Salisbury Plain? Shouldn't they be doing something brave somewhere?' I asked Bob.

'Watch, learn, and admire.'

I grabbed the biscuits from my ration pack to dunk in my coffee and lay back on the canopy of the truck with Bob for a good view. The Hercules was on its approach again, with the flap down at the rear, and the spotter planes were either side of it, taking photos. What followed was quite extraordinary.

A few objects dropped from the back of the plane and, after free falling for a while, three small parachutes opened above each of them to allow the objects to have a smooth landing. As the one I was focusing on got closer to the ground, I noticed it was a small vehicle, which Bob said was a Ferret or a Fox, I can't remember which. An animal nickname, anyway.

This happened a few times and the vehicles always landed way over by the dropping zone. 'What has this got to do with the SAS?' I asked, baffled.

'How do you think those vehicles get out of the back of the Hercules?'

'I guess they're pushed out on a static line,' was my best guess.

'Wrong. They're *driven* out by the SAS. They're testing the parachutes to see if you can drop a vehicle with a driver into a war zone so that, when they land, all they have to do is disconnect the parachute and they're instantly mobile.'

Wow! As the Hercules approached again, I watched in absolute awe and tried to fathom out whether this was an act of complete bravery or utter madness. I never came to a conclusion, but I did shower them with respect on the return journey.

26/ Silence in church

I am ashamed to say that, during my six year army career, I never completed one full Remembrance Service without being escorted out of church and being ordered to wait outside. It is not something I am proud of and I would also like to add it is also not something I had any control over. I now know it's a phenomenon neuroscientists have studied. To anyone reading this who is cursed with nervous laughter, it may ring a bell but, to anyone else, I will sound like a heartless young woman with no respect.

Everything always went well until faced with the one-minute's silence. It is an involuntary and immediate reaction but, when I'm in a space with a lot of people all being silent, I have a compelling urge to giggle. I don't for one minute think it is funny that hundreds of thousands of men lost their lives and it saddens me to think that the likes of my granddad and my dad have seen atrocities I can't even begin to imagine. However, any sense of sadness or reality just doesn't come into it and, for reasons I cannot explain, but which scientists can, whenever there is a one-minute silence, I get a deep-rooted urge to giggle that is so strong it just takes over me.

My first army experience of Remembrance Day was the worst. In full uniform, we were marched to the local church in a squad. I had a remarkable feeling of patriotism. I was next to Dotty in church and we sang the hymns and listened to the prayers. It was all very emotional. That is, until they asked us to remain silent for one minute.

I don't know what happened but, within seconds, I could see Dotty's shoulders rising and falling and I knew she was having difficulty holding back a giggle. Although I couldn't hear anything, it was contagious and, with my eyes watering, I too felt the hysteria forming deep in the pit of my stomach.

Panic set in and I tried desperately to fight it, but it was too late and, with Dotty giggling next to me, I had no chance. Now, I don't want to seem like I am whining, but Dotty started laughing first yet I was the one getting jabbed in the back by the RSM's cane. Of all the places in church that the RSM could have sat, it had to be right behind me. The more he jabbed, the more I flinched and jumped, which meant the more I giggled. The more I giggled and jerked around, the harder he jabbed and the more Dotty giggled and we just seemed to feed off each other.

Through clearly gritted teeth, he suddenly spewed, 'Outside! Now!' There was a distinct threat to his voice that made me almost too scared to leave the safety of the church. It was hard enough to stifle our laughter, but

Dotty and I shuffled out of the church with the RSM hot on our heels.

Once outside, the nervous giggles gained momentum and we were crying with uncontainable laughter. As I looked up and saw the RSM's face, I was helpless. His cheeks were puce and there were veins in his forehead that seemed to be pulsating. He was clearly absolutely furious. He made us stand to attention and told us to wait until the service was finished.

For the next 25 minutes, we stood to attention without speaking a word to each other. When we got back to the barracks, we were given a stiff bollocking. How lucky we were the matter wasn't taken any further.

The next year, they took precautions to ensure the same incident didn't reoccur. They made sure Dotty was at the front, in the right-hand pews, and I was at the back, in the left-hand pews. The first part of the service, again, went without incident. I was feeling confident I would make it through the whole service and then, suddenly, bam! There it was... the one minute's silence. I don't know why I did it, but I automatically looked over to where Dotty was sitting and it was like Moses parting the sea. The crowd of churchgoers in between the pair of us seemed to move aside, leaving a clear channel for me to see Dotty. She was looking right back at me.

The giggles hit immediately, intensified by someone in the church breaking wind. We didn't even wait for the RSM to escort us out, we just rushed from the church with our heads down and hoped to God that no-one thought we were being disrespectful. Once outside, we erupted with laughter as the tears rolled down our cheeks.

The RSM waited until the minute's silence was up before he came out to us. We stood to attention as soon as we heard his voice. This time we were not so lucky. We were put on a charge for insubordination and given three days' restriction of privileges (ROPs). We were excused from Remembrance Service parades from then on. Even when we were posted to different military bases, we were given duties which coincided with the service. I can't speak for Dotty, but I was definitely relieved.

I had my own minute's silence and didn't get the urge to giggle once.

27/ Never judge a book...

A small group of American soldiers came over for a month from Germany in 1985 and a similar sized group of our guys went out to Germany so there was excitement in the air again. They flew over in a Chinook and I had been detailed to drive the pilot, Captain Bilco Spragg. I drove to the officers' mess and, seeing the American uniform coming down the stairs, I got out of the car and opened the passenger door for him.

'Hey, Ma'am, y'all are getting in the wrong side of the vehicle,' he said in a southern drawl. God, he was handsome.

'Good morning, Sir, I was opening the door for you,' I responded, all very professionally.

'OK, let's cut the bull right away. Please, if you are going to be my driver, you must call me Bilco.' What a wonderful man. I knew I was going to enjoy driving him around the place. I don't know what it is about the US Army everyday uniform, but it is so sexy. Maybe it's their laid-back attitude or the accent, but there is something about a GI. I fully understand why so many women gave themselves up to the Yanks during the Second World War when they came over to the remote villages in the UK. They have an air of excitement and horniness about them.

When I dropped him off to his boys later that day, one GI stood out from the rest. He had the most gorgeous skin I had ever seen. It was a beautiful creamy caramel colour and his eyes were incredibly dark and deep. He came over and asked if he could take me out on a date. I tell you, the man was a vision and I have no shame in openly admitting that I bragged and gloated to anyone who would listen that I had a date with him.

For maximum effect, I asked him to come to the WRAC accommodation block to collect me so I could really show off to the girls. I know what you're thinking and, yes, I did sink to a level that I'm not proud of, but I was young and foolish. What more can I say?

I took extra time getting ready and made sure I looked and smelled my best. I waited patiently for my beau to arrive and sweep me off my feet. There were about twenty girls in my room, all peeping out from behind the curtains to get a good look at this mystery American GI who was to be my date.

The sound of hysterical laughter coming from the window alerted me. Giggling myself, I pushed my way over to see what was causing the infectious laughter. The sight was horrific. This could not be happening to me.

Some of the girls were now on the floor in uncontrollable fits of hysteria. I could barely believe my eyes. The gorgeous hunk of a GI had turned out to be the complete visual opposite out of uniform. Without the army hat, he was bald on top with a hairstyle resembling a monk's. He was wearing brown, half-mast dungarees (seriously?!), and a pink, I repeat pink, roll neck. And that wasn't the worst of it. He was wearing socks and sandals. Could there be a bigger crime against fashion?!

There was no escaping the forthcoming piss-taking by the girls but, right now, there was no way I could keep a straight face amidst their raucous laughter. I could barely see for tears and my face was burning with shame. Yes, karma was, indeed, a bitch. It served me right for thinking I had netted a Ferrari when, in fact, I had a custom-sprayed Reliant Robin awaiting me.

After some fast negotiation, I paid one of the girls to go to reception, offer my apologies, and explain I wouldn't be able to make our date due to the fact I was ill. I then spent the following month avoiding any calls from him and dodging behind bushes whenever I saw him approach. As I was Bilco's dedicated driver, this was extremely difficult to do. They had a big BBQ the night before they left which I avoided, choosing instead to have a night in, bulling my boots. I vowed I would never make the same mistake again.

Others, meanwhile, continued to have problems getting bulling off to a fine art. We were chilling in the block one day, generally teasing the hell out of each other. We suddenly heard a very loud "whoosh" sound coming from the far end of the corridor where a girl called Taff was. Donna, Lani, and I all raced down to see what the noise was. As we burst into Taff's room (no knocking required!) the sight before us was just too much.

She had been in the middle of bulling her boots and, being Taff, she was very thorough and quite a perfectionist, whatever the task. When she bulled her boots, she didn't skim over them like many of us would; she took a pride in it.

It all went horribly wrong when she flicked the lighter into action. Instead of loading the polish onto the toe of the boot and then putting the heat of the lighter under the toe, she had attempted to try a new method, deciding to put the lighter under the tin of polish, thus softening it up to make it easier to spread onto the toe cap.

Polish being highly flammable, it didn't react well to the heat and the lighter caused a minor explosion, which left her face, bedding, the wall, bits of the ceiling, and clothes covered with black boot polish. There were ten seconds of complete silence whilst we took in the mess before we erupted with laughter.

'Bugger off, you lot! Go on, get out!' she yelled, trying to get the situation under control. That only made us laugh even harder. 'Bugger off, you bastards,' she added, now half chuckling. For the following half hour, we alternated between teasing Taff and trying to help her clean up the devastation that was her bed space. Had this been the age of the mobile phone, photos would've gone viral on the internet.

We did the best we could, but it took her a couple of days to get the polish off everything, including her face.

If there was one thing Taff most definitely possessed, it was a good sense of humour. Had her experiment been successful, the joke would have been on us.

28/ On the ramp…age

It had been a quiet week for driving details so we were on vehicle repairs and general vehicle cleaning duties. Most of us were in the midst of a NAAFI break when Judy, one of the lance corporals, said she wanted to steam clean the engine on the Land Rover she had been working on. She was a lovely-natured girl, but wasn't the sharpest tool in the box.

She asked if someone would guide her onto the ramp. We all put our heads down and pretended not to hear her as, in the blistering heat, any job seemed like too much effort. Of course, being a lance corporal gave her the authority to nominate someone. She chose me and Dotty. This in itself spoke volumes for her sharpness. Everyone knew that Dotty and I were not to be trusted with something like directing a vehicle onto a ramp.

Not able to refuse an order, we moaned our way out of the canteen to the ramps she had strategically placed outside, wide enough apart for a truck. I instructed her to drive to the base of the ramps and stop, so I could position them. She had caught me on a "serious" day and I repositioned the ramps so they were aligned with the wheels of her Land Rover. Dotty was standing in front of the vehicle ready to direct her up the ramp.

No-one questioned why she had chosen to stand there yet, when the vehicle hit the ramp, the driver would only be able to see the sky, but it gave Dotty something to do. Judy started revving the Land Rover with maximum revs — deafening — and commenced the climb onto the ramps.

She made it to the top of the sloping part and edged her way slowly towards the flat section. When she got near the edge, Dotty shouted for her to stop. Judy carried on coming forward. Dotty shouted louder. Judy kept on coming. Half laughing and half panicking, Dotty screamed, 'For God's sake! Stop!' Judy kept on coming. 'Stop, ya daft cow!' Dotty wailed again.

There was a thud as the Land Rover's front wheels overshot the end of the ramp, rendering it stuck. Hysteria hit me and Dotty and we cried uncontrollably with laughter. Judy got out of the vehicle. 'Why didn't you stop me?'

'You what? Are you bloody deaf or something? I yelled about five times for you to stop,' Dotty snapped. Judy was flushed scarlet. Everyone in the canteen had heard the commotion and come out for a look and, as a result, she was now surrounded by raucous laughter. Dotty and I wandered off in a desperate attempt to calm down.

I don't know what it is about the heat of the sun, but it tends to make you lethargic and the slightest little thing can seem very funny. We wandered over to the Land Rover Dotty had been working on and decided to take it to the wash down area for a clean. Maybe a drop of cold water was just what we needed to bring us back to our senses.

Dotty got into the vehicle, turned the steering wheel to a full right lock and then hit the accelerator. I remember the stupid expression on her face as she stared out of the passenger window and proceeded to do a full semi-circle, crashing right into the front of the vehicle that was parked four spaces away from where she had started. I stood there for a moment, my mouth gaping wide open, staring in disbelief at what I had just seen.

She knew exactly what would happen when she locked the steering wheel, but heat craziness had its hold on her. She got out of the Land Rover and we both stared at the broken front grill of the one she had just hit.

Dotty parked her vehicle back where it had been and we walked into the office to report that a vehicle had a broken grill. That was the end of that and we went off to wash her Land Rover, still laughing.

The heat really does do strange things to a person.

29/ Party girl

With my next posting looming around the corner, I was offered a move to Rheindahlen, which I promptly turned down. Some of my friends thought I was crazy as the posting came with a promotion to lance corporal.

I loved the idea of Germany, but there were two main reasons preventing me from taking it. Firstly, Rheindahlen was a predominantly lesbian posting which didn't float my boat. Theoretically lesbians weren't allowed in the army in those days, yet we all knew Rheindahlen had more than most. I have nothing against lesbians in the slightest, but it stood to reason that a camp full of lesbians meant less room for men and those odds didn't sit comfortably with me at all.

Secondly, what was the point in taking a promotion to lance corporal when I seemed to be constantly in trouble for something? I figured they wouldn't be able to rip my stripe off my arm if I didn't have it in the first place, so I gracefully declined and spent the best part of my career kicking my own arse for being so stupid. You shouldn't knock something until you've tried it. I mentally put a lesbian affair on my bucket list, should there become a shortage of men.

When my posting came up to Clattenhall Barracks in Kent, I was excited and gutted at the same time. I cried all the way there and, believe me, it's a long way from Wiltshire to Kent when you're unhappy. It was, however, amazing how much stuff you could fit into a Datsun 120Y when you packed it tightly. A lot of the girls hated a new posting as it made them anxious and nervous, but I absolutely loved it, apart from leaving terrific friends behind. For me, it was a chance to start again with a blank canvas — a whole bunch of brand new colleagues and new routines.

As this was my second posting, I knew roughly what to expect of the job, but the rest was uncharted territory. I was a little apprehensive too as I was going to be unfamiliar with the area which, as a driver, could be a little stressful. There was no lovely satnav lady back then to tell you which direction to turn either.

I arrived on a Sunday and my roommate was to be a lovely girl called Pam who was really sweet and helped me settle in. She took me across to the cookhouse on the Monday morning for breakfast and, as I turned to sit down, I saw a girl from my home town. We kind of grew up together although she was a couple of years younger than me. Mel looked up. 'Bloody hell, Lorna, what are *you* doing here?'

After a quick introduction and ten minutes' catching up as old friends,

I felt much more positive and able to fit in with this new set of girls. I can't tell you how good it felt to see Mel, as being the new girl on camp made you stick out like a sore thumb. She herself was pretty striking with long, wavy blonde hair, hazel eyes, freckles, and incredibly long legs, particularly given she was a few inches shorter than me. Mel was the icing on the cake of my day. Or so I thought.

After breakfast, we were sitting chatting when the duty warrant officer walked into the cookhouse and made his way over to one of the tables to talk to someone. I actually felt a tugging in my groin when I saw him; he was a pure vision... an Adonis. Who *was* that guy? I later found out his name was Sergeant Major Dorset.

With his olive skin, ebony hair, and big dark eyes, not to mention the all-important wings on his arm, he was by far the icing of the day. Maybe the cherry on top too. That very moment, I promised myself that, at some point during my stay at Clattenhall, I would have a slow dance with that man. Of course, there was one small hurdle — he was a warrant officer and well beyond my reach.

Life in my new MT troop soon settled and laughter was on the daily menu, but there was a part of me that was missing. Dotty had been posted to Lulworth in Dorset. I missed her, particularly as my 21st birthday approached after I'd been at Clattenhall for a couple of months.

Since being posted there I'd only drunk tonic water at the NAAFI. Being the new girl, I didn't want to make a fool of myself until I got to know my peers a little better, so I didn't drink for a couple of months to keep a clear head.

My first night back on the booze was to be my birthday night, the 21st of May, 1985. The block was buzzing and the weather was great. Everyone's windows were open and you could hear the sounds of stereos blasting tunes from different bunks and rooms. Yes, the party had already started in the girls' accommodation.

I was so looking forward to this night as this was the mother of all birthday celebrations and I was going to enjoy every moment of it. The poison of choice amongst the girls at Clattenhall appeared to be sangria so I thought I would start with a bottle of the ready-made stuff, closely followed by a litre bottle of Pimm's. I glugged both neat on the rocks as I presumed that was the correct method of consumption. Whoops. How was I to know that even the sangria mix was meant to be diluted with lemonade?! Finishing off with a couple of cheeky bottles of Henry Funk beer, we all made our way over to the NAAFI where Mel ordered two pints of tarantula, a heady mix of cider, blackcurrant, and Pernod.

Taking our drinks to an empty table, we sat down and our banter flew freely. We'd probably been there for an hour or so when the strangest thing happened to me. I had no control over the motion whatsoever, but I started to slide sideways off my chair. I actually passed out before I hit the floor. The time at this point was about nine o'clock and, prematurely, the party was over for me. I have no memory of what happened after this point.

I woke up the following morning on top of my bed, fully dressed and still proudly wearing my party hat and streamers. According to everyone in attendance, my party had been a raging success. I felt robbed. Clattenhall was the place that taught me how to pace myself when drinking beverages of the alcoholic kind.

Despite my new-found prudence, I loved the come-as-you-are parties that only happened on stomp nights. Someone would burst into the rest room or into your bunk and announce what kind of party it was going to be. The first you would know of the party would be "shipwreck night" or "toga party" being bellowed at around four o'clock. You had to use all your initiative to scrape together a costume that would relate to the theme of choice, often only having a couple of hours to do so. You'd regularly see a crowd of uniform clad girls bursting through the doors of the Oxfam shop, all frantically searching for appropriate clothing.

Shipwreck night was easiest as you just had to shred the bottom of your shirt and trousers, put on a bandanna, a patch over one eye, and a large hoop earring through one ear. Toga nights were always a little risqué as you were aware someone may rip off your bed sheet if you hadn't tied it securely. On toga evenings, I was always a little more guarded and never quite let all my inhibitions go. Some cheated and wore shorts underneath so that, if their sheet did get ripped off, they were respectable. Spoilsports.

On one occasion, Tessa and I decided to go dressed in something completely different. It wasn't an official come-as-you-are party, but rumours had spread that the two courses of lads would be attending in fancy dress. We decided to go dressed as the Blues Brothers. We didn't tell a soul what we'd planned and somehow we managed to muster up a black trouser suit each, with a black tie, and pork pie hat. We already had the dark glasses so we were good to go. By nine thirty we knew the NAAFI would be in full swing.

We'd pre-arranged with the DJ to play the Blues Brothers theme tune a few minutes later and made our way over to the double doors of the stomp. The minute we heard our tune, the spotlight was on the double doors and we burst into the NAAFI in full Blues Brothers kit. There was an eruption of cheers and we made our way over to the bar to a series of pats on the back and smacks on the bum. It was a very successful night indeed.

Dotty would've loved it. I desperately missed my partner in crime.

30/ The troubles

During the '80s, the troubles in Northern Ireland were still very real although not as prominent as they had been a decade earlier. This meant that any regiments going over on a tour of Northern Ireland needed to be suitably trained. For a small part of this training, they came to Clattenhall Barracks, which required volunteers. Northern Ireland training was a real hoot for us drivers and the easiest duty of all time.

The army had built an entire street in the middle of waste land. It had been named Albert Street and, in all its splendour, resembled an average street in the heart of a troubled area over in Ireland, or so I was informed. There were Sinn Fein posters hanging from windows and the walls were plastered with anti-army graffiti. As part of the training, our squadron had to pair up and act like residents of the street, living in the houses.

Some of the houses had weapons concealed in hiding places within the building. We even had Royal Ulster Constabulary (RUC) officers drafted in for the training. The lads raiding Albert Street were part of a regiment which was due a tour of Northern Ireland. Some of this training was to experience the kind of hostilities they might face whilst on tour.

The poor misguided buggers were in for such a shock when they hit Albert Street. Our instruction was clear and simple — give them as much shit as possible. For some reason, Northern Ireland training was always in the middle of the night and followed a stomp, so the majority of the so-called Irish civilians living in the houses on Albert Street were drunk as skunks. That may or may not be what they could expect for real. How hard could it be?

Along with the regiment in training, there was a requirement for a WRAC called the "coffee pot" to be present, the term used for the female soldier in the crew. She was in place for one reason and one reason only — to be present when there were any females or children in the building that was being searched. On entering Albert Street, the team would line up flat against the wall of the house and the member of the RUC would knock on the door, wait for an answer, and then burst in whilst reeling off a speech which included that they had a right to search the building.

Now, if it was a really cold, wet day, the civvies inside the building would get a bucket or bowl and fill it with a horrendous mixture of anything they could get their hands on, including cold tea, coffee, and a few cigarette ends thrown in for good measure.

One of the so-called residents would be waiting upstairs by an open window and the minute they heard the knock on the door, they tipped the contents over the poor unsuspecting beggars below and shouted, 'Sod off, you army bastards,' or something similar, usually involving the F-word. This would severely piss off the soldiers in the team and make for a much more realistic night. However, we had one bunch of marines who didn't see the funny side.

As soon as one of our girls, Clarise, opened the door and started to run upstairs, hot on her tail was a very wet and bedraggled marine with a major sense of humour failure. He reached out, grabbed her hair, and pulled her down the stairs, breaking her collarbone. For this regiment, it was the end of the exercise and the unit were sent back as course failures.

From the marine's point of view, I could see it probably seemed unnecessary to throw dirty water and cigarette ends at him on a freezing cold night. If, however, you put it into perspective, whatever we put these lads through on Albert Street was nothing in comparison with what they could actually face in Northern Ireland. If they couldn't keep their heads with the training dished out on Albert Street, then for sure they were not ready to head off for the real thing.

31/ Witch-hunt

As the WRAC accommodation was a women-only building, I don't need stress the fact that men were absolutely forbidden. If you ask me, this was a rule that was just made for breaking. I was dating TC, a guy who looked a little like Colonel Abrams, the singer, who was deemed hot at the time. After a very drunken Friday night, we ended up back at mine. Whoops.

One heady night of passion later, I woke up ridiculously early with a mouth like the bottom of a birdcage and decided to put the kettle on for a brew. As it was around five o'clock on a Saturday morning, it was no surprise that TC was still in a deep sleep.

I threw on some shorts and a T-shirt, grabbed the kettle, and made my way to the ablutions to fill it. The journey there from my bunk was approximately 30 paces but, during that short walk, I noticed a few things that were definitely out of the ordinary. For a start, at that time of day, there were far too many people up and about. I then noticed they were all non-commissioned officers (NCOs) who were lance corporals and corporals and they were buzzing. To top it off, I saw people I'd never seen before, including a couple of very official-looking men.

Panic rose in my stomach like bile and I broke out in a sweat. As casually as I could, I made pathetic small talk and muttered a greeting to the men whilst on my way to fill up the kettle. The journey back to my bunk was somewhat quicker as I'd come to the conclusion it was a dawn raid on our accommodation to find out who had men in their rooms. I got back to mine, shoved the kettle on the chest of drawers (tea was now the furthest thing from my mind) and looked at my bed.

TC was sprawled out, naked as a jaybird, with an erection he could have used to pole vault to safety. I had to wake him with the minimum of noise and get him out through the window.

I placed my hand over his mouth and gave him a shove. To say he woke up panic-stricken and fighting was an understatement. There followed a brief struggle as I tried to calm him and he fought me off, thinking he was being attacked. I briefed him on the raid and told him to grab his shit, make like a banana, and split. As he quietly but rapidly got dressed and his proud erection reduced to something resembling a Walnut Whip, I reached for the blind in order for him to make his escape.

I noticed there were three further people I'd never seen before outside, lined up against the wall either side of the window belonging to the bunk next to mine. TC was going to have to stay for now.

Petrified, I stepped away from the blind, convinced they were after TC. I couldn't think straight and had no idea what to do with him. Although I could think of one thing, now was clearly not the time!

I decided a cup of tea was needed after all. TC was in a frenzy so I told him to get into the wardrobe whilst I thought what to do. Remarkably, he did as I asked and I made the tea, handing him a cup in the wardrobe.

Nothing made sense. The NCOs knew that Sandy in the room next to me was a lesbian and, therefore, would be the last person to have a man there. Why did it look like they were going to raid her room? Did she know they were going to do it? I felt sick that I couldn't warn her.

I sat down on the bed and tried to make sense of it all. If they were going to raid the room next to me, then maybe I was safe. They couldn't possibly be looking for men.

Suddenly, it hit me and I felt myself relax a little. They were doing a dawn raid all right, but not for illegal blokes in the block. It was a lesbian hunt as they weren't allowed in the army, although we reckoned about 60 to 70 per cent of the women were lesbians. Ultimately, I didn't care if you were lesbian or straight. I do, however, humbly apologise to all my lesbian friends for being so relieved it was a raid to catch them and not men but, in a crisis, it's every man for himself if you'll pardon the pun.

If I could have warned Sandy, I most definitely would have as we were all WRACs at the end of the day. It was a sisterhood.

Once the raid was over and the officials had left the scene, it was rumoured that, if you'd taken an aerial view of the accommodation block, there would've been men running for their lives from every possible fire escape, window, and exit.

A valuable lesson was learned that night — never let your man stay for a sleepover.

32/ Little monster

Of course there were times when the odd bloke found his way into our accommodation unaccompanied, usually drunk and having been elected by a group of guys on a dare. On one occasion, a man did just this, although I can categorically guarantee he never tried it again.

There were periods in the army when we were totally skint and desperately waited for pay day, just like in any other job. When those hard times hit, we would unite on a Saturday and put what little money we had into a central pot. Once we had counted the contents, off we went to purchase four or five loaves of bread, some Mattesson's liver paté (and it *had* to be Mattesson's), and a selection of horror videos. A toaster materialised in the lounge area and, whilst one girl was in charge of toasting the bread, another took care of spreading the paté on the toast and passing the slices around. A happy little family.

I don't know why I tortured myself watching the horror films because they really did traumatise me. Apart from the fact I watched most of the film sweating from behind a cushion, when I had to return to my room on my own my imagination came into its own and scared the shit out of me. During one of the films, in the darkness I noticed a spider run across the floor. So as not to alert anyone to this discovery, I casually raised my legs and sat on my feet. Lani followed my eyes, saw the spider and was onto me in a heartbeat. She was up and made straight for it.

I felt sick with panic as, bad as my phobia was, I became a little unpredictable if threatened. At this point, the other girls were aware of the situation and it was pandemonium. Some screamed and ran around the room or tried to get out whilst others sat frozen to the spot. So much for us being tough army girls.

I tried to remain calm as if I didn't care, but Lani wasn't buying this at all. She walked over to me, her hands cupping the spider, and asked if I wanted it. Panic gripped me and I was up and making for the door yelping, 'Get stuffed, Lani,' with her hot on my tail. She was grinning at me and I can honestly say that, had I been in possession of a loaded gun, I felt as if I wouldn't have hesitated to shoot her to prevent her getting anywhere near me with that spider.

I opened the door and ran into the duty room. Lani was in pursuit, backing me into a corner. I begged her to go after someone else, even naming a couple of the girls who were just as scared, if not more so, than me. Yes, that's right. I sold my friends down the river. I was petrified.

Her hands shot out towards me and I saw something black heading for my chest. Everything seemed to be in slow motion and I couldn't tell if it was dead or alive, not that this made a difference. She turned to run, but fear now had a hold of me, and I grabbed her jumper and dragged her backwards. I no longer knew where the spider was, but my fear had surpassed worrying about it. I was mid panic attack and wasn't thinking straight.

Lani fell backwards onto the floor and I have no memory of the couple of minutes that followed. I just remember being brought back to the here and now by Judy, the duty corporal, screaming at me to let Lani go. I looked down at Lani and found myself straddling her, my hands placed either side of her head. I had been banging her head on the floor. Judy dragged me off her and I could see blood on the floor. I was confused. I had no idea where the blood had come from.

Clarise led me from the room, and Judy stayed to check Lani over. I must have blacked out with fear and lost the plot. I started to cry when Clarise told me what had happened, and kept repeating, 'I'm so sorry.' Clarise was incredibly sweet to me.

'Don't worry, pet, Lani has a head made of cast iron so it would take more than a clout to damage her.'

I appreciated her light-heartedness, but stood up and made my way to the duty room. Lani was sitting on the bed with a glass of water in her hand. For a split second, she looked worried but, once she saw I had been crying, she relaxed. I walked over, grabbed her in a bear hug and started to cry again. I apologised again.

We sat and talked in the presence of the duty corporal and she explained to Lani how severe phobias can be. I, on the other hand, was told to get some therapy to get over my fear of spiders. Luckily, the cut on her head was only small and no further treatment was needed. After a 30-minute break, we reassembled in the living room and continued with the horror movies.

After the final film had finished, *Zombies of the Lake*, the light went on and my prickly, sweaty feeling started to fade. Most of the girls thought the films had been crap and I sure as hell wasn't going to let on they had frightened me half to death. Normally Lani would be the one to leave a little earlier to hide somewhere, ready to jump out, make you scream and want to punch her lights out for scaring you. I made my way back to the safety of my bunk, hearing distant screams as Lani (completely un-phased by the early evening's events) did just that to someone. I had a feeling she wouldn't be scaring me any time soon.

My imagination was already running away with me and I hadn't even got into bed yet. The minute my door was closed, I heard a voice in my head. *Check the wardrobe, you can't see a poltergeist so it could be anywhere.* By the time I needed to turn off my light, I was terrified of my own shadow. I put one finger on the light switch and positioned myself so I could just switch off the light and dive straight into bed, pulling the quilt right over my head until I had calmed down slightly. I tried to reason with the voice in my head by reminding myself it was just a film, but I just couldn't shake my fear.

Suddenly, I felt the quilt move and my body became instantly alert again. The hairs on my neck and arms stood on end and, in an instant, my entire body was prickled with sweat. I didn't move or even breathe for a minute as I fought with my imagination, sure I was just being paranoid. I lay absolutely still but… shit, it moved again. I wanted to cry. Something was under my bed and it wasn't Lani. Oh, how I wished it were Lani.

I noticed how silent the block was and began to think everyone else had been murdered already and I was the last one alive. I froze as the quilt moved again. I had tears in my eyes and I couldn't have moved if someone had placed a gun to my head. I held my breath, too afraid to breathe. The rush of blood around my body was so great my face was prickling and my vision blurring.

Suddenly, without warning, a hand grabbed my ankle and I screamed. I flung back the quilt, jumped out of bed, made for the door, and ran down the corridor, screaming that there was someone in my room. Within seconds, the girls appeared in the corridor with various weapons: rounders bats, boots, and empty wine bottles.

The stupid ass bloke who had been under my bed appeared and was laughing his head off whilst staggering down the corridor, pissed as a fart. The girls went in for the kill, battering him with everything they had. He sobered immediately and sped towards the door, falling over twice on the way and taking an extra battering from the girls.

We convened to the living room to stay up for another couple of hours, laughing at how sore he would feel in the morning. My laughter wasn't quite as carefree as the others. I was still reeling from the shock. It really was one of my worst nightmares and it was going to take a while to get over.

33/ I dare you

As you may have gathered, I was no shrinking violet and seemed to court trouble whether I wanted to or not. I could run from it, but I couldn't hide and felt as if I had an invisible magnet about my person that attracted trouble. Not terrible trouble, but mischievous trouble.

Whilst drinking in Mel's room one afternoon when we couldn't afford to go to the NAAFI, some bright spark came up with the idea of playing spin the bottle. It seemed like a really good idea at the time.

We sat down in a circle and Tessa spun the bottle. When it stopped, it was pointing directly at me. Not halfway between me and anyone else, just directly at me. I wish I'd been this lucky with expensive-prize raffles but, if this had been a raffle, I guarantee it would've pointed elsewhere. After much deliberation, one of the group threw in the idea of me running naked around the perimeter of the accommodation block as a dare.

Most people would at least stop to think it through or try and barter for a different dare, but not me. No, Sir, I was already whipping my clothes off, desperate to prove I was a party animal. I was encouraged to embrace the moment thanks to the chorus of "Get 'em down, you Zulu warrior" from the girls. I suspected nothing. I was up and making for the front door, eager to get the task under way. Bearing in mind our accommodation block was adjacent to the cookhouse, which was still open, it was alarming I had no inhibitions whatsoever.

I opened the door, a little put off by the chill in the air, and took off at a jog to complete my lap of honour. I heard a few cheers coming from the NAAFI and the cookhouse, but didn't bat an eyelid. When I'd completed the lap and arrived back at the front door, the bastards had locked me out, clearly a plan that had been hatched during my run. I banged on the door and the whistles and cheers just increased as the crowd had gained momentum.

It was a sobering moment and the girls on the other side of the glass door howled with laughter. It was annoyingly contagious and I couldn't help but join in. I turned around, gave a bow to my audience and Mel opened the door to let me in. It was freezing and I had nipples like chapel hat pegs.

I never played a game of spin the bottle again during my time in the military.

34/ No place to hide

Occasionally as a driver you could be given the most boring driving details. Having to drive someone somewhere and wait there all day in the Land Rover was one of the worst. Too uncomfortable to sleep, too cold to walk around outside, you just sat there all day.

Then again, sometimes you landed the detail that made joining the army as a driver worthwhile. Pam and I had been told we were going on exercise to Tarnworth Woods. Oh, what joy! We finally got to play real soldiers and have guns. They didn't trust women with guns very often, a smart move as far as I could see — a premenstrual woman with an attitude, a grudge, and a loaded gun was surely a recipe for disaster.

We picked up our old MK trucks and were each allocated a troop of men to drive out to the woods. We had collected our camouflage equipment and had our mess tins and tea mugs (we knew how to prioritise!) all packed and ready. We were absolutely buzzing as we were the only two girls on the exercise so, if we worked it right, it should be quite a relaxing couple of days and we should get first dibs on the food and the tea.

We were en route to the woods and spirits were high. It made it more interesting for some of the guys if there were women on the exercise as they could show off a little and puff out their chests. Sexual innuendos were forthcoming and the atmosphere was brilliant with Pam and I giving as good as we got. There's nothing quite so refreshing as a bit of flirty banter. Ultimately, it makes the world go round. It's nothing sexual, just flirting. A little like the *Carry On* films — smutty but harmless.

We parked the Land Rovers, the men went off to do what they had to do, and Pam and I camouflaged the vehicles and strategically rubbed a little camouflage cream on our faces for good measure and full effect. We knew we would regret it later as the stuff was a nightmare to remove and left you with seriously unattractive blocked pores. Usually after an exercise, it took two or three showers and then a soak in a hot bath to erase the cream. I hope that's improved in the last 30 years if nothing else.

We were starting to look like real soldiers now. Truth be told, we looked more like Rambo in drag, but we were definitely looking less girly than we had.

We made a brew and read our newspapers. Within the hour, the novelty of dossing had worn off and, after a while, boredom set in. We were scheduled to remain in position all night so the hours ahead were looking bleak and very long indeed. Our problem was that the guys were all away playing soldiers with guns and we were left by the trucks doing absolutely nothing.

Well, that wasn't exactly true as we were on stag guard duty with a light machine gun which meant we were to ward off any attackers, even though we were highly unlikely to get any. Even as a non-combatant corps, we were still trained to use guns and were ready and waiting, with blanks rather than live rounds, whilst we lay in the truck, the machine gun on a tripod beside us.

The company sergeant major (CSM) returned to base and we began to nag. We refused to give in and were now begging for him to let us take part in the exercise. Although we'd been provided with a gun whilst there, at no point would we get to use it so it may as well have been made of clay.

'Sir, please let us go on tonight's ambush,' Pam begged him.

'We won't make a sound and no-one will even know we're there,' I whined. He fought his corner really well, refusing to give in, and then faltered momentarily and we lunged.

Had he just sternly said, 'No,' we would probably have given up. Instead, he began to list the feeble excuses as to why he didn't think we should take part. He had a weak argument and we used this to our advantage. It was as easy as taking candy from a baby. He knew he had lost the argument and just stood, looking helpless. It was in the bag, we were on tonight's ambush whether he thought it was a good idea or not. What was the worst that could happen? We were in the middle of Tarnworth Woods in Kent, for goodness' sake, so how dangerous could it be?

As night fell, the woods got eerily dark and spooky and the lads weren't making it any easier by telling us scary stories — not funny. Pam laughed at everything and no story phased her, whilst I was petrified because I knew these stories would come back to haunt me when I was alone.

We split into our teams and huddled down together in the undergrowth. The exercise was being carried out in autumn so the woods were full of dry twigs and crunchy leaves so even a nosy field mouse venturing out for food sounded like a T-Rex on the prowl.

The night was quite frightening and already the stories were beginning to cloud my judgement. Once in position, we weren't allowed to smoke or talk and breathing was restricted. It seemed like we were in that position for an absolute age when, in actual fact, it was probably just short of an hour.

Without warning, the calm and quiet were obliterated. Not the crunching of a leaf or the cracking of a twig. We were thrown into pandemonium. All I could hear was shouting and various scuffles breaking out.

I was completely stunned. It was almost as if everything was in slow motion. One minute I was sitting in the bushes and, the next, I was being dragged through the undergrowth and pinned against a tree by someone who was knee high to a Woodbine, his elbow jammed against my throat. This in itself was an achievement given I'm just over five foot ten.

I had received scratches and probable bruising to various parts of my body, my beret had been knocked off in the scuffle and, to top it all, my windpipe was severely restricted because some bastard had me pinned against a tree, shouting in a language that wasn't English. Well, it didn't sound English to me, although I hasten to add that I am no linguist.

My hair unravelled from its bun when my beret was knocked off, leaving it partially hanging down my back. As it turned out, having long hair was to be my saving grace. As soon as the bastard with his elbow lodged into my throat discovered I was, in fact, a female soldier, the whole scenario shifted. I was released and further chaos broke out. The little man was now shouting what appeared to be commands to his men and became involved in a heated discussion with our CSM. Pam and I were pumped full of adrenaline and, although still in shock, fired up and ready for round two.

It emerged we had been ambushed by a Gurkha regiment, which would explain how they had managed to attack and capture us without a sound. It was like being ambushed by the Predator. When we returned to camp, we discovered the Gurkhas were uncomfortable man-handling a woman in an aggressive manner, and somebody was in for a shedload of trouble for it. We never did find out exactly what happened, but the CSM got called up in front of the CO.

I had a few experiences with the Gurkhas, mostly involving drinking in the NAAFI, and they could knock back rum like it was water. I have nothing but respect for these people as they sometimes went for a year or more without seeing their families. To them, it was a great honour to be part of the British Army and they were extremely proud of their role.

With the exception of the incident in the woods, they were nothing but courteous, well-mannered, and smiley. They were *always* smiling.

35/ One false move

A number of commandos came on course to Clattenhall and Mel and I became great friends with a guy called Bluto. He was a gem of a man and we loved the bones off him. He was like the brother I had never had. The three of us, together with his mates, Doc and Psycho, laughed until we cried. Mel and I socialised with them on many occasions, but the real bond I had was with Bluto; there was just something very special about him. I loved him like a family member and thought the world of him. He was a Scouser, a great laugh, hard on the outside, but very soft on the inside. When their course came to an end, I was devastated.

They made their way back to Plymouth, where they were based. Bluto and Psycho invited Mel and me there for a weekend not long after they had returned. We couldn't resist the invite and had a terrific time. Union Street was our favourite — yes, full of pubs.

A few weeks later, we were invited back for a replay. Bluto had promised to get a couple of barrels of scrumpy jack and it was going to be a blast, apart from the fact we didn't have enough money to get to Plymouth and back. We'd left it so late to tell the boys that we were too cowardly to pick up the phone and let them know our situation. I knew Bluto would be upset we'd let him down, but he was a good person and he would have understood. Instead, we buried our heads in the sand and avoided all calls. A stupid course of action on our part as this started a ball rolling that would have major implications on their military career.

Bluto and Psycho consumed the whole barrel of scrumpy, stole an army Land Rover, drove to Dover, dumped the vehicle, jumped on a ferry to France, and joined the French Foreign Legion.

We didn't realise what had happened for some time. The first we knew about this was through a postcard that arrived two months after our aborted weekend. It was from an alias, not signed by Bluto, but there was no mistaking his handwriting. He used calligraphy and his writing was like a piece of artwork in itself. The guilt we felt at being responsible for this turn of events was crippling. If only we had called or borrowed the money, they would still have been safely tucked up in Plymouth. Now they were somewhere in France and AWOL from the British Army.

Over the next few months, letters and photos arrived from the same alias. Naturally, when I received a letter with photographs inside, I looked at the pictures before I read the letter. My heart almost broke when I saw the state of the accommodation they were living in. It was like a dirty old barn and the floor was rough and filthy. Towels hung over cobbled walls, bearing the French Foreign Legion motif. The last photograph in the pack made me laugh and cry at the same time. It was a picture of Bluto in his Foreign Legion uniform and kepi, wearing his trademark grin. He was such a giggler.

I proudly showed the photos to a couple of close friends and you would've thought they were photos of my non-existent husband receiving a knighthood the way I was clucking. I felt so proud. I settled down to read the letter. My bubble of happiness was well and truly popped. Its contents shocked me to the core and, yet again, I wished we had gone to Plymouth that fatal weekend.

He described a punishment received by one of his colleagues for insubordination. The poor lad had to dig a one-metre-square hole in the ground. It was the middle of winter and the ground was solid. Once he had dug it, he was commanded to stand in the hole whilst the rest of the men were ordered to take it in turns to punch him in the face. I was horrified.

Their training was coming to an end and Bluto and Psycho were due to be shipped out once they'd finished it. Now was the time to make up their minds whether they were going to stay in the Foreign Legion or escape and make their way back. They didn't know where they would be shipped out to, but it could be anywhere in the world. The letter didn't say whether they were going to stay or leave so I just had to wait.

A few weeks later, I received the news they had arrived back in Plymouth. It was months before Bluto called me. It had taken them seven days to make their way back to Britain, sleeping in the bushes by day and travelling on foot by night.

Once they returned, they were arrested and charged. Bluto received a six-month sentence at Colchester Military Prison and was stripped of his rank. It was touch and go whether they would remain in the army or be dishonourably discharged. His commanding officer stood up for him and explained that, not only had he been trained by the British Army as a paratrooper and a marine, but he had been trained by the Foreign Legion too which made him a very highly skilled individual. That saved his neck.

36/ Losing a special friend

Bluto and Psycho eventually both received a posting to Clattenhall and we resumed our friendship. Nobly, they forgave us. Not long after, Mel was posted to Northern Ireland. I was incredibly sad she was going and also quite envious as I had applied for a tour there. A few things prevented me from being able to go. A female soldier had to have a clean record, which I clearly didn't have due to numerous charges, and my father's side of the family were all devout Catholics and may have been very pro-IRA. I wasn't religious at all but, even so, it wasn't deemed safe for me to go.

Just as I was recovering from the loss of Mel's company, disaster struck again. Bluto had met a local girl and proposed to her. I couldn't believe it. The ink was still wet on their first date menu. He had neglected to tell me he'd proposed, but news travels fast on an army camp.

I was having a drink in The George on the Saturday night after hearing the news and decided to drown my sorrows. Unbeknown to me, Bluto had decided to go there. After a couple of drinks, I was feeling somewhat better. Until Bluto walked in.

For some crazy reason, I was overcome with emotion and ran out of the pub in tears. Bluto was hot on my heels. He grabbed me, spun me round, and told me he loved me, always had, and all I had to do was say the word and he would call it off with his fiancée.

I loved this man with all my heart, but as a brother, not a lover. I was 21 years old and just having fun. He was 30 and ready to settle down. I wanted to tell him I loved him and would marry him tomorrow, but I wasn't going to make a commitment I couldn't be true to. Not to him, he deserved better.

So I stood, sobbing like a baby, and very much caught between a rock and a hard place. If I told him I was in love with him, I could stop him marrying this girl he had proposed to out of loneliness, but if I said I wasn't in love with him, he would marry her and I would lose my best buddy. What a predicament.

'I'm so sorry, Bluto, I can't say the word. I'd be lying if I told you I was in love with you.' I had said it out loud and I felt lousy. 'I love you as the most special of friends, but I can't commit my heart to you forever.'

'OK,' he croaked, clearly devastated.

I sobbed my heart out as he went back to the pub. Sadly, we spoke very little after that. I really missed him and felt as if I had lost a limb. Why couldn't I give him what he wanted? He was the perfect guy: a great sense of humour, would walk over hot coals for me, put me before anything else, and truly loved me. Life was so unfair. Why couldn't I reciprocate his feelings?

37/ Up, up and away

A few months later, I began seeing Tully, a guy who had been on Bluto's original course. He was an extremely good-looking lad and his only flaw was that he was a real player. Our relationship was casual, no strings attached. Bringing up the rear of my happiness was lady luck ready to give me a swift kick up the arse. I fell pregnant.

Two things that most definitely would not work in unison were a female soldier and a baby. During the following couple of weeks, whilst I worried how to break the news to Tully, I miscarried. Part of me was desperately sad but, in all honesty, a larger part of me was relieved. I was barely able to look after myself, let alone bring up a child as a single parent.

I was under no false illusions where Tully was concerned — he was a ladies' man and that was what had attracted me to him in the first place. Well, that and his smouldering good looks. I decided it would be best if he didn't find out, which would save embarrassment all round. Luckily, his course ended almost immediately after the miscarriage and he returned to his unit, our relationship very much over.

The following weeks were empty without him and I felt the void. I was terribly down after the miscarriage and felt as if I cried for two months solid. I decided I needed something to occupy my mind and, along with a girl I'd recently befriended, booked myself on a course. Anita and I initially thought it might be a giggle to take a parachuting course but, after much deliberation, decided against falling out of planes and secured places instead at a gliding course at Bicester.

My sister and brother-in-law were both in the Royal Air Force (RAF) and were members of the Cranwell Gliding Club. They were solo glider pilots and I'd been to the gliding club on a number of occasions and even flown in a glider. Once you had conquered the vertigo (which I suffered with miserably) it was an exhilarating experience.

The rest of the girls soon got fed up with us talking constantly about the course and we both remained confident it would be a doddle, despite people's horror stories. For some reason, people didn't have a lot of confidence in us completing the course. I wonder why…

The weeks flew by and the big day arrived. Our excitement was unreal. I don't know if we were more excited about the fact we were going on a gliding course or whether we were just excited we were escaping camp for a week. We arrived at Bicester and were shown to our accommodation. From there, we were taken to the cookhouse to be fed and watered. Oh boy,

RAF food was so much better than army food. A night ahead in the gliding club was on the cards and we had decided to make a conscious effort to remain sober as we had a big day ahead of us.

We met our instructors who were members of the RAF and very posh in comparison to their army counterparts. There seemed to be a significant difference in maturity between squaddies and airmen. Even so, I still preferred a squaddie. They seemed rougher round the edges perhaps but, to me, they were more men's men, ready to rough it whatever the circumstances.

We were here for a whole week and we were determined to have a great time, hopefully returning as solo glider pilots. It wasn't really the type of licence I needed but, what the heck, it was a further licence to add to my list.

The following morning was beautiful. The weather was gorgeous: the sky blue, the sun shining, and the air was fresh. There were a few white, fluffy clouds scattered about the sky and we were so ready for this course we could taste it. We were transported to a field where various gliders were dotted around. They really were a sight to behold. So sleek-looking I couldn't take my eyes off the wings. Jeez, they were so long!

There was also a double-decker bus parked in the field, which struck me as odd. It was soon explained that this was the chuck truck. The bus provided tea, coffee, and an array of food for everyone, which instantly cheered us up as we hadn't been provided with a ration pack at breakfast and we had an awful feeling we were supposed to go all day with nothing to eat. After a cuppa, we went to the classroom for the theory side to becoming an accustomed glider pilot.

I have to confess that this theory part of the course was mind-numbingly boring and I found it difficult to concentrate. I was later to learn that, as boring as the theory may have been, my subconscious had understood more than I could have believed. After a very long and dull session, the theory side of things was over with and we were allowed back into the field.

Finally, it was my turn and I was called over to the glider. I could barely contain my excitement and was obviously too pumped full of adrenaline to realise my excitement was, in fact, a grisly disguise for fear. In my effort to impress the RAF, I had completely forgotten my fear of heights and flying. It only struck me as a very handsome man fumbled between my inner thighs, attempting to fasten a parachute.

'What's this?' I asked.

'A parachute, just in case,' he replied, smiling. My mind was spiralling out of control. *In case of what?! Why is he fitting me with a parachute? Are we going to crash?* I didn't know the whereabouts of the ejector button as we hadn't learned that in the theory.

'I don't want a parachute and I don't want to go up in the glider any more,' I muttered under my breath. Either he didn't hear or chose not to pay me any attention. I looked at the glider and noticed that a horrible, sinister smile with big teeth had been painted onto its nose, giving it a "say your prayers, honey, your ass is mine" kind of look about it. I opened my mouth to tell this gorgeous guy I had changed my mind and was afraid of flying, but all that came out was, 'Thanks.' Pathetic. I was going to die that very day in that glider and all because I didn't want to look like a fool in front of the good-looking glider man.

I forced myself to take a grip of the situation and opened my mouth to protest again. I did much better this time. 'Am I flying with you?' *Oh, for the love of God, get a life!* This was neither the time nor the place for flirting. *What does it matter how good-looking he is, he will be dying with you in said glider.*

I looked at it and was sure the sinister grin had widened. *But, of course, he won't be dying, will he, because he knows where the ejector button is and knows how to work a parachute...* As I didn't have the bottle to end this nightmare, I bravely stepped up to the glider and made for the back seat.

'You're in the front,' said the handsome man. Great, I was to get a bird's eye view of my crash landing. The most frightening part of the flight was the takeoff. I would later discover it wasn't so bad if you were towed by a small plane, but I can confirm that taking off via a winch was horrendous.

It required a person to hold the tip of the wing to keep the plane level and, when the winch began to haul it in, this same person ran with the plane whilst keeping hold of the wing. As the plane got faster, the wing was abandoned by the runner as they were unable to match the speed of the plane.

It was very noisy as you were bumping across the surface of the field when suddenly, without any warning, you shot up towards the sky with the wind whistling through the wings. When you got to a height you could maintain without the winch, you pulled a lever that disconnected the winch and you were at one with the sky. If you could get over the initial shock of the takeoff, it was well worth it.

I checked my parachute straps again as a precaution to make sure I was ready for anything. Now that we were in the air, Nigel (as all pilots seemed to be named) started sharing his flying knowledge with me. It was so quiet up there and the view was breathtaking.

We soared around the sky and I asked a multitude of questions. Any thoughts of crashing were long gone and I was having the time of my life. It seemed as if we'd only just taken off when we were coming in to land.

I'd taken the controls whilst we were flying and was amazed at how light the "stick thing" was — my technical knowledge was clearly still a bit lacking. It was as light as power steering. We landed and I climbed out, shaking all over with the adrenaline rush and feeling very pleased with myself.

Anita was up next and I wished I could have gone straight back up again in her place. However, I was needed for much more important things. I was to become the wing holder and would be running with the aircraft on takeoff. It was more difficult than it looked as you had to run at a fair pace to keep up whilst trying not to trip over grassy mounds. After a stint at running up and down the field holding the glider wings, I was offered a cup of tea in the chuck truck. I gratefully accepted.

By day four, I was starting to really get the hang of flying. Nigel showed me how to find a thermal and fly within it, which gave the glider the ability to gain height. I had managed to cover almost all the items on my checklist and I considered myself well on the way to becoming a solo glider pilot. The checklist was part of a log book and listed all the different moves you perform during training, which we ticked off along the way. I had only one thing left to overcome — the solo flight.

The following morning was the big day and we were so nervous. I'd already looked in my log book to check that nothing could go wrong. I scanned down my checklist: takeoff — check; landing — check; cable break — check… ish. I had a brief flashback to my experience of a cable break. I didn't actually experience this but, on one flight, we released the cable prematurely which is a kind of simulated version and I coped OK. Well, apart from the frightening experience of the loud, clanging thud as we released ourselves and the sudden jolt similar to major turbulence, that is. What could go wrong?

I arrived at the airfield excited and full of emotional adrenaline. I had my ritual cup of tea and then my moment had arrived. I was ready for my maiden flight. I felt like James Bond and I think my approach to the glider may even have been in slow motion. The feeling of anxiety and fear mixed with adrenaline and power. I had never felt so nervous. I approached my glider and climbed in. I covered all my checks and the roof came down. The winch was attached and the runner was to my left, holding the wing.

I was so scared, I thought I might throw up. I could hear my own heartbeat and had a sudden mini panic attack and wanted to get out of the plane. I had left it too late. Oh, God, what the hell was I doing? Suddenly, I was jerked back to reality and the winch began to reel me in. It was all too late now and I was going to have to give it my best shot.

As we thundered down the field, bumping in all directions, I glanced at the runner and noticed the strained look on his face. I wondered if I'd pulled the same face when I had been in his position. I must have spent a while thinking this because I suddenly noticed the runner had disappeared and I was leaving the ground. I pulled back on my lever as I'd been taught and we rose to the heavens. All my previous excitement vanished and I had my serious, flyer's head on now.

The one thing I hadn't taken into account when I eased back on the lever was that the weight in the glider was now different to previous flights as I was a man down. This thought hadn't even occurred to me until I got to about 100 feet and heard a ridiculously loud banging sound, at which point I nearly lost control of my bowels. 'What the hell was that?' I shouted out loud. Fear whipped through me like a deadly poison and I had a quick thought as to how much safer the parachute course might have been after all.

I remember looking out at the scenery and seeing what a beautiful view I had. I could see for miles and it was such a gorgeous day. There were sheep in a field below, grazing without a care in the world, and I spotted some horses. Everything seemed to slow down around me and the glider quickly levelled off. The only explanation I have for what happened following that loud bang is that I must have gone onto autopilot. I have no memory of any thoughts or actions that I had or took.

After seeing the horses, I came to with the thud of the wheel hitting the grass. I have no idea how I landed or whether I followed the correct procedures. It felt like a large amount of good luck to me, but one thing I was crystal clear on was there would be more chance of me having lunch with Elvis than there would be of me attempting a solo flight again for as long as I lived.

I came to a halt and sat there in stunned silence. Panic crept over me and I felt emotionally wobbly yet too paralysed to cry. I've no idea how much time passed before my instructor and a couple of other fellow gliders appeared by the side of the glider, but it was probably around ten to fifteen minutes as I had landed three fields away. It felt like an eternity.

My instructor was smiling and very excited. Could he not see my face? Was it not obvious that I'd been scared half to death and was now in the middle of a sense of humour failure?

The lid popped open and everyone was so excited, all babbling at the same time, making it impossible to hear what anyone was actually saying. I felt a pat on the back as I managed to force my shaky legs out of the death trap. My instructor was talking to me, but nothing he was saying registered. It was as if I no longer understood English. I could see his lips moving, but I couldn't understand a word.

The whole situation seemed a little surreal. We left the glider with the other people who had joined the pilgrimage to the crash landing site and made our way back to the field.

Nigel was still talking when suddenly my ears resumed partially normal service. '…get you on the bus and get a sweet cup of tea… get you up again in an hour for another go... ' was all I could make out. I stopped dead in my tracks and looked at Nigel like he had just grown a second head.

'Are you kidding me?' I was in no mood to impress this guy any more and didn't hold back. 'There are two hopes of getting me into any glider ever again and one of them is Bob,' I said very firmly. ("Bob" being our rhyming slang for "no hope". Bob Hope, no hope.) 'As far as I'm concerned, this morning's experience was a message and I can confidently say end ex. Thank you for your time and patience and for having faith in my ability. I bid you a fond farewell.'

Luckily for me, after watching my solo flight attempt go horribly wrong, Anita had now decided she really didn't need a solo licence after all, so it was end ex for her too — end of exercise. She insisted on driving me back to camp because she didn't think I was quite over the shock of the morning's events. I had provided her with an excuse to get out of her solo attempt. And that was the end of our gliding course. I never did make it to solo pilot, but considered myself very lucky to be alive.

I break out into a cold sweat when I think of landing that day as I still have no memory of it at all.

38/ A likely story

Several months later, I was sitting in the NAAFI on a Sunday evening, having a quiet drink with Tessa and idly watching two guys playing pool. Studying one of the guys more closely, I noticed it was Tully. I couldn't believe it. He must have felt me staring and looked over. I smiled, he blanked me, and carried on playing pool. 'Did you see that, Tessa? Tully just blanked me completely,' I said, totally bewildered. I was now on a mission to attract his attention just to prove a point.

Every time he looked over, I smiled and he blanked me. About an hour later, he eventually came over. 'I think you may have me confused with my twin brother,' he smiled. *Yeah right, a likely story. God, he is such an ass.*

'Your twin brother?' I asked in a mocking tone.

'Yeah, I have a twin brother called Joe. I'm Bo Tullyman.'

I didn't want to believe him, but he did seem different — quieter and kinder. It turned out he was telling the truth. He told me his wife had been the girl next door and it was a natural progression they should marry. He also said that, if it hadn't been for his daughter, he would have ended the relationship some time ago. I know what you're thinking and, yes, I'm a sucker for a sad story, but I wasn't completely taken in by all this talk, it just seemed irrelevant. I didn't care if he was married or not, nothing to do with me.

For the entire six week course, we spent every spare moment together, both alone and with his friends. Such a different experience from my time with his brother, Tully. Bo was nowhere near as brash and loud as his brother who had the gift of the gab and could've sold snow to Eskimos.

Tully gave me a warm and fuzzy feeling, but I was under no illusion — he was such a ladies' man and party animal. His constant flirting with other women had often made me feel worthless, humiliated, and hurt, yet I'd been too besotted to walk away.

Bo, on the other hand, had a deeper attitude to life and, when he asked me questions, I knew he listened to my answers. Out of the two, spending time with Bo was a much more pleasurable experience and not just a physical relationship like I'd had with his twin.

I only told Bo about the miscarriage with Tully's baby about three weeks before he left. He was really angry I'd gone through it by myself, although the choice had been mine not to tell Tully.

During Bo's final week on course, Tully came back on a two-week course himself and the brothers spent a couple of nights out on the lash. We hadn't told Tully we were in a relationship and, as I was in my room one evening getting ready to go out, Tully sneaked himself into the block and made his way there. He was incredibly drunk and clearly thought he would just pick up where he left off.

I told him what an ass he was, shoving him down the corridor where I promptly opened the fire exit and threw him out. I felt much better after ejecting him from the block, but regretted not telling him about the miscarriage. For some reason, I wanted to hurt him as badly as he had hurt me with his womanising, but he was drunk and it would have meant nothing to him. Who knows, it may have meant nothing to him had he been sober, so I'm glad I didn't tell him.

Bo flew into a rage when I told him about my visit from his twin, but I told him to leave it given Tully had been drunk.

I was devastated when Bo's course finished and missed him terribly when he left, but we'd agreed not to keep in touch as it would've been pointless. He was, after all, still married.

39/ Test drive

I had to wait until my last summer at Clattenhall before I finally got my chance to dance with the very gorgeous Sergeant Major Dorset. It came on a Thursday night at the stomp which was heaving with people as it was an end-of-course "do" and three courses were ending instead of just the one. Most of the guys and their instructors had come in fancy dress and the NAAFI was buzzing. We drank and danced the night away and the atmosphere was brilliant.

As the DJ slowed things down with Phyllis Nelson's "Move Closer", I was making my way back to our table but, before I was off the dance floor, I felt a tap on the shoulder. I turned round and there he was, the Adonis, the god of all sex gods.

'Shall we?' he asked, his head slightly tilted to one side and a twinkle in his eye. I was dumbstruck and just nodded. His arms went around me and our bodies locked as we began our slow dance. He smelled gorgeous and some of the girls looked over in complete shock, but I was beyond any help and lust was making me high as a kite. I think it may have been that summer is a bit of an aphrodisiac too.

No one man should be given that much sex appeal and be so out of bounds to any woman. It was just criminal. We stayed on the dance floor, locked together for a couple more, slow dances — Champaign's "How 'bout Us" and Atlantic Starr's "Secret Lovers". It was clearly meant to be…

And then the evening was over. The lights came on and I expected him to disappear into the crowd. In all honesty, those few dances would have been enough for me and I could quite happily have walked away a very happy woman.

Once the NAAFI closed, a group of us made our way over to the WRAC's accommodation block and sat outside on the grass, chatting and laughing in the summer evening's warm air. Tessa had the great idea of going to get the sin bucket, a bucket we kept especially for these occasions. Everyone had to bring all their alcohol and pour it into the bucket so we could all dip our cups in. I guess it was the army version of a punch bowl.

Looking back, it sounds disgusting but, when you were already a little drunk, it was a wonderful idea. We all disappeared and re-emerged a few minutes later with what alcohol we had. As it got tipped into the bucket, you couldn't help but wonder what it was going to taste like. There was whiskey, sangria, beer, vodka, and Malibu to name but a few.

As none of us had thought to bring a cup with us, we were now trying to nominate someone to go and get one. No-one had even noticed Sergeant Major Dorset approach with a few of the other instructors so we were all silenced when he walked up to the bucket, cupped his hand into the mixture, and drank. You would think he had just invented the wheel from the way we all stared at him in awe.

Someone threw a few plastic cups out of their window and we fuelled up. It didn't take long for the liquid to recede to the bottom of the bucket. I don't know what it would've tasted like if I had been sober but, from a slightly drunken point of view, it was just fine.

Sergeant Major Dorset leaned over towards me. 'My place or yours?' There it was, just like that. The simplest of questions that set my head into a spin cycle. My heart was pounding so loudly I was half expecting the girls to get up and dance to the beat. I quickly scanned the faces of the crowd to see if anyone had heard him, but no-one seemed to have noticed anything untoward which made me think I'd just imagined it in my slightly drunken state. I just stared at him. He leaned even closer and asked me the same question again. I hadn't imagined it.

'Yours,' was all I could whisper. There was no way I was going to take him to my room with all the girls listening at the door. A couple of the girls looked over at the pair of us as we were sitting very closely. When he stood up and held his hand out to help me up, I felt very light-headed indeed and off we went in the general direction of the sergeants' mess, hand in hand.

The situation was completely mad. He was a sergeant major and I was a private. This sort of thing should just not have happened, but I was under his spell and powerless to stop myself. I was reminded again just how good he smelled when the evening air caught his scent.

The sergeants' mess was strictly out of bounds on a social level to a mere private like me so he had to sneak me in, which just added to the excitement. We were both more than aware we weren't exactly going to his room for a game of Scrabble. I felt like a teenager again and wasn't even sure I would remember what to do when we got to his room so I hoped he would take control of the situation. Once inside, it was a relief when he poured us each a glass of wine. After a few sips, I realised how disgusting the contents of the sin bucket had been.

My nerves were on fire and I was shaking slightly. I slugged down the wine in the hope of finding some Dutch courage or, indeed, courage from anywhere. I'd only taken a few gulps when the glass was taken from my hand and his lips were on mine.

I was light-headed again and almost prayed I wouldn't pass out. It was a hard and passionate kiss, his tongue exploring my mouth with urgency. I wished I hadn't had the cheese and onion crisps at the beginning of the night and hoped he couldn't taste them. As we thrashed around the room in the throes of passion, clothes were ripped off and we stumbled into the furniture.

Suddenly, he broke free and told me to sit down on the bed whilst he prepared a surprise. My mind reeled. Oh, dear God, I was going to have sex with a sergeant major in the sergeants' mess. What was I doing? Everything spun and I tried to imagine what he could possibly do as a surprise.

He didn't disappoint. I was sitting on the bed, tensed up, with my eyes closed as commanded and, let's face it, I couldn't refuse a direct order from a sergeant major. That was an insubordination charge in itself.

'OK, open your eyes,' he said in his incredibly deep, sexy tone. The sight before me was one I will never forget. There he was, standing with one foot on the floor and one foot on the bed, wearing only his maroon beret, a smile, and a very impressive erection. This was one sergeant major who knew how to stand to attention. A perfect ten in my opinion.

Once I had taken my eyes away from his weapon of mass destruction, I scanned the rest of him and, wow, he looked so fine with a stunning six pack and his beautiful tanned skin. I'd never really noticed just how sexy a maroon beret could be, or maybe it was because it was worn as part of a package. It was all too much to cope with.

I stood up and lunged at him. As we stumbled around the darkened room, locked at the lips, our hands were all over each other. After my fingers had wandered and savoured every part of his toned stomach, they headed further south. Even after all the alcohol he'd consumed, he was hard as a rock and, once again, I felt slightly faint and hugely impressed.

Our kiss intensified, we lost our footing, and landed on the floor. His mouth left mine and traversed over my body and the scream I let out could surely have been heard by someone in the building, but we were past caring.

Once again his mouth was on mine. My heart could barely cope with the pace of the beat, he was pure dynamite. We stood up and crashed into the chest of drawers. Somewhere in the distance, I heard something smash, but didn't think anything of it. He picked me up like a rag doll and I straddled him willingly. I screamed again when he entered me. I didn't think I could hold it together for much longer.

Our movements were so frantic that momentum had now somehow taken us onto the bed. Our bodies glistened with perspiration and we were breathless, but still couldn't get enough of each other. With all the thrusting, we slipped from the bed onto the floor. The fall did nothing to slow us down and we thrust and moaned like two wild animals until we could take no more and climaxed simultaneously.

It was like the life energy had been drained from us as we lay slumped in a heap. I opened my eyes and noticed the clock on the wall said it was ten past four. We had been making love for the best part of four hours.

My senses slowly returned and I wondered how bad the carpet burn was on my back. The fact it was hurting was a clear sign I was beginning to sober up a little.

After what seemed like an age, we were up and back on the bed with our arms and legs entwined. We said nothing for a long period and I realised we'd never really had a conversation before. He was five ranks higher than the two rank legal limit you were allowed to date within and I was aware I had to get out of the building at some point without being seen.

As I turned to nuzzle into him, he gazed at me and his lips were on mine again, only this time not as hard as before. We kissed slowly and passionately whilst exploring each other's bodies, which aroused me again immediately. Slowly he moved on top of me and gently entered me. I was sent straight back to paradise again. I met his every thrust, all the while staring into his dark eyes.

I wondered if any one moment in life could top this feeling of euphoria that I felt right then. For a stolen moment, I truly believed I had fallen in love with this guy and we could live happily ever after. This time, he climaxed before me and, instead of collapsing, we stayed intertwined for some time just looking at each other. It was around five thirty when we eventually fell asleep.

I woke up with daylight streaming in through the window. My head was fuzzy with an acute hangover. As my eyes began to focus, panic hit me like a knock-out punch from Tyson as I wondered where I was. I was aware someone was behind me and I prayed for no nasty surprises.

I slowly turned my head and, when I saw Sergeant Major Dorset sleeping behind me, so intense was my fear I thought I would throw up. Questions screamed through my head. *What the hell am I doing here? How on earth am I going to get out of this little mess? Lorna, answer me that!* I carefully lifted his arm and placed one of my legs and one of my arms on the floor.

What followed is difficult to explain, but involved me trying to slide out of bed without moving any covers and required some very controlled moves. It was like a really bad game of Twister.

It took me nearly fifteen minutes until I was sitting on the floor, trying to absorb the state of the room. The furniture was crooked, the lamp was in fragments, the glasses and the wine bottle were smashed, and there were torn clothes all around me. I began gathering up the remnants of my clothes and noticed there were no buttons left on my shirt. Brilliant.

But I had a bigger problem. I couldn't see my knickers. I couldn't find my bloody knickers. Despair hit again and I refused to leave without them. As I looked up to the heavens for guidance, I spotted them on top of the wardrobe, half on and half hanging off. I stood up to retrieve them.

'Surely you are not leaving so soon.' I knew my face was crimson with embarrassment before I even turned around and, when I answered, I seemed to have lost my normal powers of speech.

'I n..n..n..n..need to go b..b..b..b..before anyone gets up.' Stupid answer, but it was all I could manage. I was hungover and my body felt like I had been beaten.

'But I'm already up,' he said and pulled back the covers to reveal another killer hard-on. Bloody hell, the man was a machine. 'Come back to bed or I may think you were just using me,' he chuckled.

My sense of responsibility now decided to make an appearance and remind me this man was way out of my league. I felt awkward, vulnerable, and very foolish. Not so foolish, however, that I wasn't prepared to have one last go on the merry-go-round before I left. I climbed back into bed and awkwardly avoided eye contact with him whilst he showed me once again how incredibly fit and sexy he was.

Although his performance was astounding and I still found him incredibly attractive, the situation somehow now felt wrong. I realised perhaps he had been right — I had just used him.

The entire love-making session was spent with my face a lovely shade of crimson and I was all fingers and thumbs. Once we were finished, I prayed he would dismiss me and allow me to slither back to my room for a shower. All I could hope for now was I would never have to face him again.

As I dressed, he stood up and said he would see me later. I was wise enough to know he would most definitely not see me later and was just being polite. No doubt I would never see him again on a sexual level and, truth be told, I was gutted because I knew I may never top that sexual encounter.

I ducked and dived out of the building and was relieved to be in the clear. I ran and didn't stop until I made it safely into our block, only to be met by Lani. 'Bloody hell, you look rough, girl! Good night, was it?' she grinned.

I shrugged and headed for a shower. Soon I felt a little better and decided to put the whole experience behind me, although I tingled all over every time I thought of our amazing night together. At least I had the memory of it, albeit somewhat hazy. The good-humoured comments I received from the girls I took on the chin. I realised I would be yesterday's news before I knew it. I just needed to keep out of Sergeant Major Dorset's way.

The detail board, however, had other ideas...

40/ Crossing the line

My name was on the board. Placing my finger alongside it, I ran it across to see who I would be driving that day and, to my absolute horror, it was Sergeant Major Dorset. A wave of nausea came over me and Lani, having seen the board first, burst out laughing as the enormity of the situation hit me.

'Round two,' she winked. I was far from seeing the funny side. I was mortified and set about asking all the girls if they would swap details with me. No-one wanted to as it was an all-day job and, being a Friday, everyone wanted to knock off early. I was doomed.

I collected my Land Rover and made my way to the field engineering wing. The walk down the corridor seemed endless and Sergeant Major Dorset's office was right at the end. A couple of the sergeant majors who also worked there were a good laugh and yet I was dreading walking in. I hesitated outside the door as I could hear laughter coming from the room and, for a moment, paranoia told me they might be laughing at me. It's odd how suspicious you can become in these situations.

I bit the bullet, knocked on the door, and mumbled that the transport for Sergeant Major Dorset was outside. 'Come in and take a seat, he isn't ready yet,' said Sergeant Major Ellis.

'Yeah, come in,' came the distinct voice of Sergeant Major Dorset. I walked in and sat down. The intense heat coming from my face indicated I was crimson again. Luckily they spared me the jibes about how warm it suddenly felt, but Sergeant Major Dorset kept giving me sly winks when no-one was looking. I felt inferior and foolish, but I couldn't deny him his incredible good looks. There was no doubt the man was a stud muffin and I secretly longed for a repeat of the previous night.

Throughout the day we made small talk and he said he wanted to see me again, but we had to be careful because of his rank. A couple of sneaky kisses were grabbed during the day and he said he would call me.

His call came on the communal phone in the block where anyone and everyone was likely to answer it. Unfortunately for me, it was Lani who answered. I tried to tell her she must have been mistaken when she rushed into the living room announcing that Sergeant Major Dorset was on the phone for me. The room was packed, but she was having none of it because she said she had recognised his voice.

I approached the phone with an air of coolness on the outside and a knot of fear on the inside, with a dozen or so pairs of eyes watching on from the living room door. 'Hello,' I said, trying to sound casual.

'Hi, how are you fixed for tomorrow night?' he asked.

I began to shake. 'Yeah, fine. What time?'

'I will pick you up at around six.'

'OK, see you tomorrow. Bye,' I whispered. That was it! I was in for another heady night of passion.

Six o'clock the following day came round quickly. I so needed a drink before I met him. I couldn't do this sober, he was a sergeant major for goodness' sake. I told the girls I was going for a drink with a guy on a course and they all believed me bar Lani. That girl could smell a rat from a mile.

I was on edge, hanging around the front door trying to look casual, but probably looking very suspicious. I spotted the car turning the corner and was out of the door and down the steps as quickly as I could. The cookhouse was right opposite and there were a few stragglers still in there from the evening meal. I couldn't understand why he was being so open about this. It was as if he didn't care who saw him.

We went for a drink and then parked up so we could look down over the Medway and see the lights of it twinkling away prettily. We made love in the car and talked. It was the first time I had actually had a conversation with him. We discussed what we would do if we won the football pools — these days we'd be fantasising about winning the National Lottery — and the places we would travel to together. I told him about home and he talked about his career. Roughly four hours later, we headed back. Instead of dropping me at the block, he headed for the mess again.

'Where are we going?' I asked.

'Back to my house for the weekend,' he told me casually. I felt a bit on edge should anyone see us entering, but excitement once again overruled the situation. I couldn't fathom out how this guy was single. Once inside, he opened a bottle of wine. He put on a Luther Vandross album and we danced naked in the living room in candle light and, when the dancing turned into kissing, he picked me up and carried me upstairs.

We had a wonderful night and, in the morning, he made me breakfast in bed. It was surprising how well we got on and just how genuinely nice he was. I knew the relationship could go nowhere because of his rank, but I didn't waste time thinking about it.

We remained naked all weekend and spent our days eating, making love, and bathing together. It was quite honestly the best weekend of my life thus far. On Sunday evening, we dressed and he drove me back to the block.

The following weekend I had arranged to meet him in The George. It seemed to be general knowledge amongst the girls that we were seeing each other, but it was like the elephant in the room that no-one talked about. A taboo subject.

Whilst I was getting a drink, Doug made his way over. He was a real slimeball no-one really liked. If he had to be anything but human, he would most definitely be a snake or a weasel.

'Word has it you're shagging a sergeant major,' he leered at me.

'Go play with the cars outside, Doug.'

'You do realise you can get kicked out if someone was to report you, don't you?' he jibed.

'Sorry, Doug, but you seem to be mistakenly under the impression that your opinion is of any interest to me,' I told him, without even bothering to look at him.

'Well, how d'you think your precious sergeant major shag buddy would feel if you two got reported?'

Luckily for me, at that very moment, my "shag buddy" walked into the pub and heard the threat. Doug hadn't seen him so I looked him right in the eyes as I said, 'Well, I don't know, Doug, why don't you ask him yourself?' and nodded behind Doug. The colour drained from his face as he turned around to face my "shag buddy".

'Do you have something to say to me, Corporal?' my Adonis asked.

'No, Sir. Of course not, Sir,' he could only mumble.

I continued to see Adonis for a few months before it eventually petered out. It was a wonderful relationship and I do sometimes wonder where his life took him.

Meanwhile, life in the army carried on as usual and courses and men came and went.

41/ A madcap idea

I am not proud to announce I went AWOL during my army career. At the ripe old age of 22, I thought it was a terrific achievement as I didn't exactly always take army life seriously, did I? But the wisdom of many more years on my mental clock makes me cringe in shame at what I got up to on that occasion.

Long after Mel had been posted to Northern Ireland, Anita and I were fed up with never being able to get to use the equipment in the gym next to our accommodation due to the amount of guys posing on it. There never seemed to be a time when the machines were free and, young and easily intimidated, we weren't keen to use the gym when it was full of men.

I think we were, in fact, a little fed up with army life in general as we'd recently done a lot of evening details and weekend duties. We fancied some time off to go shopping so we decided to go AWOL. I don't know what our definition of the army was at the time, but the fact we wanted a day off to go shopping made it clear it wasn't a very realistic one.

We sat and planned the whole event and the rush of adrenaline was overwhelming. We booked a cab for four in the morning to pick us up outside the sergeants' mess as we thought we would live dangerously. Start as you mean to go on. Although we didn't know exactly where we were headed, we took a train to London.

From there, we decided it would be fun to go to Latchmill for Anita to meet all my old friends. We clearly hadn't thought this through as the last place any sane person would go AWOL is another army camp.

That aside, we arrived and managed to get a room in the girls' accommodation block... through legal channels. Unbelievable, I know, but we were actually given a room. How lucky was that? We told everyone we were on a week's leave and had decided to come to Latchmill.

The first thing I decided to do was call my mum and dad to let them know what was happening as my mother was a worrier. I chose my words carefully and kept my telephone conversation to a minimum. 'Hi, Mum, it's just me. When the police come round, don't panic, OK?' I then hung up. In my 22-year-old head, that brief piece of information would rid her of all worry. In reality, off course, my mum spent the next four days worrying, panicking, and pacing the floor.

It was great to see the old crowd and we phoned Lani twice a day to get any gossip. She was running a book on the odds of us being locked up on our return. The odds were high on us being placed under arrest which, at the time, made the whole concept more thrilling.

For four days, we shopped, drank, ate take-away food, and had the most amount of fun you could have with your clothes on. Although I have to confess the clothes did come off at times too. On the fifth day, we ran out of money and decided to go back to Clattenhall to share our experience with the girls. In our minds, we were one step ahead and decided to return on a Friday evening, thus giving us a final weekend of fun before facing the music on Monday morning.

The block was fairly quiet when we returned and the girls gathered in the living room were really pleased to see us. It was terrific for around an hour. Until the duty corporal announced she had been given instructions to place us under arrest.

This was all going horribly wrong. We were supposed to have a weekend on the lash before this stage. She took us down to the guardroom, still in our civvies, where belts and shoe laces were taken off us. Crikey, the last thing I was going to do was hang myself — I still had stories to tell.

The weekend was abysmal, but my spirits were kept high by having a laugh wherever I could find one. Anita, on the other hand, had now sunk to an all-time low and was clearly regretting having ever met me, let alone having disappeared on a jolly for four days. I know I have an overpowering personality at times, but I sure as hell didn't ever force anyone to do anything so I wasn't taking *all* the blame for that.

Monday morning came around far too quickly. We were told to stay in the rest room at the MT yard and patiently waited to be called in front of the CO, who would determine our fate.

I got called first and was frogmarched in. The CO read out the offence and charge and then was stupid enough to ask, 'Do you have anything to say for yourself, Private McCann?'

My reply was astonishing, now I look back. 'I can honestly say I think the break did me good, Sir.'

He turned purple and the veins in his face pulsated as he bellowed between gritted teeth, 'I am so very glad to hear it, Private!' I got the distinct impression he wasn't at all glad to hear it.

Anita received similar treatment, though she chose not to say anything stupid to him. We were informed that, as there were only two cells for WRACs at Guildford guardroom where offenders were sent for punishment and one was already occupied, we were to be spared the jail sentence. The result was fourteen days' loss of pay and fourteen days' restriction of privileges (ROPs).

I had officially come down from my high. The raw fact was I was to lose half a month's pay and I had to look forward to two weeks of scrubbing, sweeping, and generally doing the worst manual jobs imaginable. On top of that, I had to undergo three dress parades daily at the guardroom and somehow fit in a day's work. Served me right.

42/ Dressing down

I would consider myself to be quite strong-willed and am very proud to come from a tough family. I was raised never to let anyone see you upset or weak so, when our first ROP task was sprung upon us, I smiled my way through it.

We were instructed to clean the urinals in the guardroom and cells. I cannot begin to describe how disgusting those urinals were. They had clearly not been cleaned in years and were absolutely gross, making us physically gag. The urinals had bits (I tried not to dwell on the thought) stuck to the sides with enough pubic hair to make a wig. We weren't given the privilege of rubber gloves or detergents and were to clean them with bare hands, a ripped-up combat jacket, and a bucket of water.

My gag reflex was working just fine. Men were disgusting creatures. Anita was nearly in tears and I wasn't exactly thrilled with the situation myself, but we kept up a united front whilst having a laugh with the guys on guard to hide our despair.

That wasn't the end of the job either. Once finished with the urinals, we were told to wash the windows and walls down in the guardroom using a bucket of water and yet more bits of ripped-up combat jacket. They sure had a lot of old jackets.

Every square inch of the walls had severe yellow staining, the result of decades of soldiers smoking away their boredom. Being a driver, your tool of trade was a good quality chamois leather so I asked if I would be able to collect the leather and some cleaning products from the block. Mere water was never going to be sufficient to do the job. They permitted us to run back to the accommodation and collect what we needed to complete our task.

We made a fantastic job of the walls and windows and also managed to keep a sense of humour throughout, chuckling again with the guys on duty and the prisoners. It had actually turned out to be quite a pleasant evening (if you ignored the close encounters with the pubic hair) and I think we may even have gained a little respect from the men.

The following morning, we were told to report to the RSM's office. We didn't know why we'd been summoned, but nervously made our way over to the admin building anyway. After waiting outside for the best part of half an hour, we were marched in front of him. He was a bastard of a bloke, par for the course with an RSM. There was always something very unnerving about them. This one was like no other warrant officer. He was twice as loud as the rest and a little bit like Windsor Davis playing Battery Sergeant Major "Shut Up" Williams in the '70s sitcom *It Ain't Half Hot Mum.*

Someone from the previous evening had reported back to him that Anita and I had been laughing and generally enjoying our punishment which didn't bode well with him at all. He bellowed that under no circumstances were we to be seen fraternising with soldiers again whilst carrying out our duties. If we did, we would be brought up in front of him and charged again. It's a sad day when you can't even enjoy your punishment.

I hated every minute of it and we went on to scrub out more urinals (word spread how good we were and what a grand job we made), swept the roadsides, and did a lot of weeding.

It was the latter that finally broke Anita. I pulled her to one side and told her that, when she got back to her room, she could wail like a banshee but, until then, she just had to hold it together. I was quite astounded at my own grit and determination to complete this punishment with dignity. That is, until they threw a completely new task at me, and only me. This was the quick change parade and I was to face this alone.

Parades in general meant having the state of your uniform verbally ripped apart. Although, in all fairness, it depended who was on duty. Some would see the lighter side of the situation and others were seemingly assholes on a power kick. I had never heard of a quick change parade before and, as the details unfolded, it sounded like fun. When you joined the WRAC, you were issued with the following uniforms:

- work fatigues — green shirt and trousers, khaki tie, green combat jacket
- standard female uniform — A-line green skirt, white blouse, green tie, American tan tights
- combat — green combat jacket and trousers, puttees
- NBC suit with gloves, boots, gas mask
- No. 2s — A-line green skirt, white blouse, fitted green jacket, green short tie, American tan tights, peaked cap

The day of the quick change parade was a scorcher and, although it took place late afternoon on that Friday, the temperature was still way up in the 80s. Most people had knocked off for the day and were chilling. My quick change parade started with a standard inspection of my work uniform at the guardroom. I was then given three minutes to get back to the girls' accommodation block (about a one-minute run away), change into a uniform that had been dictated, before returning back to the guardroom ready for it to be inspected.

The first run back to the block went smoothly until I got back to my room and started ripping off my uniform whilst screaming for someone to help me find my standard uniform. A couple of the girls came to assist. I very quickly briefed them with my current situation whilst changing. They said they would round up the others and be ready for the next change.

I made it back in three-and-a-half minutes as I'd wasted valuable time looking for the uniform in my closet. Heck, three minutes isn't very long when you're sweating, running, and dressing all at the same time.

With each change, news had travelled around camp and I now had an interactive audience. The girls were invaluable and, as I rounded the corner of the road, I shouted out what uniform was coming next and the girls in my room would be holding it up ready for me to run straight into.

I was suffering from heat exhaustion and, by the fourth change, I didn't give a toss and unashamedly stripped whilst running down the road past the men's accommodation block on the way back to my own. I didn't care if they saw me in my underwear. Some of the guys were hanging out of their windows, cheering me on and whistling as I ran past. The girls were all lined up with an item of clothing each and I just ran to the appropriate girl and dressed on the way back to the guardroom with another encouraging cheer from the lads.

Change number five was a bitch. I had to get into my NBC kit, complete with gas mask. 'Bugger me, Tessa, I can hardly breathe as it is without shoving a gas mask on,' I panted.

'Get it on, McCann, and show 'em what WRACs are made of,' she encouraged. I wanted to cry. Once I'd scrambled into the NBC suit, I grabbed my gas mask and made a run for it. I didn't put my mask on until I was halfway back to the guardroom as I would have passed out. There were a few shouts of "Get ya tits out for the lads" and "Get 'em down, you Zulu warrior", but I couldn't oblige on this occasion as I was just a little preoccupied. This was definitely not fun and was actually more unpleasant than the urinal task. I felt quite emotional and my eyes welled up a couple of times whilst running past.

As the little shit at the guardroom had seem me running without my gas mask on, he also made change number eight the NBC kit and told me to run in the mask. I was emotionally and physically exhausted and very close to throwing up due to dehydration. After ten changes, the sadistic bastard finally decided he was bored and called an end to the charade.

I was dismissed and returned back to the block, covered in sweat, but possibly a little fitter. As I walked past the men's accommodation for the last time, I was met by an amazing standing ovation from the lads and took a bow in my work trousers and bra. As an optimistic person, I decided to see the whole experience as a personal fitness lesson. I now needed a very cold beer.

Just one more evening parade to get through and the eight o'clock parade in the morning would be my final punishment dress parade. I would've served my time for my crime. I went for a quick lie down at eight thirty that evening and, whilst I was sleeping, guess who raised her ugly head? Lady luck's evil twin. She decided that fourteen days of being everyone's bitch wasn't punishment enough and added a final addendum.

I was rudely awoken at ten by Lani shaking me and shouting, 'Mate, you're late for parade.' Shit! Words failed me and dread tore through me. How could this happen? My last evening parade after fourteen days of sheer hell.

I arrived at the guardroom to find that the evil twin was waiting for me in the form of one grumpy, duty staff sergeant. I wanted to hang myself right there and then but, instead, I had to endure his coffee breath in my face along with the droplets of spit because, believe me, he was furious as he bellowed at me.

After what seemed like an age, I was dismissed and went back to the block deflated. On the slow walk back, I bumped into Mac, one of the lads from another squadron. 'Cheer up, Lorn, it might never happen,' he chuckled.

'Too late, it just did, Mac.'

'What's up? Not like you to be so down.'

I explained my situation and, without a moment's hesitation, he came right back at me with a plan. He told me what to say and I gave him an almighty hug to thank him. Perhaps there was a little light at the end of the tunnel.

I got back to the block and phoned Sergeant Babstock. I followed Mac's plan to the letter and explained I'd been suffering from severe period pains, taken a couple of painkillers, and gone for a lie down until they kicked in. I added they'd knocked me out, making me sleep through the alarm and, as a result, I had missed my ten o'clock parade. Sergeant Babstock was absolutely brilliant and took control of the situation immediately, telling me to sit tight and she would get back to me.

She made some phone calls, pulled a few strings, and managed to get a result. I wasn't comfortable deceiving her because we'd become good friends and I had more respect for her than I had for anyone else in a position of authority. I was also aware she was nobody's fool and probably knew it wasn't quite the whole truth, but she never let on and I guess she thought I had suffered enough. She knew me so well that, when I had gone AWOL, the CO had asked her if they should send someone to my home and she'd casually replied, 'She will be back when she is tired, hungry, and has run out of money.' She could read me like a book.

The following morning, I was called into the troop sergeant major's office where I received a lecture stating how fortunate I was to have been given the benefit of the doubt. He was old school and would never have been comfortable discussing women's problems so I just couldn't resist going into great detail about my period pains. He ended the conversation and the meeting abruptly before ushering me out of the office.

All that was left for me to do was to buy Mac a pint or three.

43/ A right pain

I was ecstatic when Dotty was posted to Clattenhall in late 1986. I had my partner in crime back. We were all getting changed for a PT lesson on a Wednesday afternoon in November. It was cold outside and we were moaning about the possibility of an outside lesson and the fact it shouldn't be allowed. We didn't know for sure it would be outdoors, but PTIs could be a sadistic bunch so it was a distinct possibility.

We arrived at the gym to be told we would be using the indoor equipment. There was an audible sigh of relief from the girls. We got the kit out including the ropes, gym horses, and climbing bars and ended up having a game of pirates. These were the only PT lessons I loved — you could have fun whilst keeping fit at the same time. The lesson passed so quickly and we were still laughing when we put the equipment away again. We usually got into squad for some cool down exercises afterwards.

Today, however, the PTI shouted, 'When the equipment is away, I want you jogging in single file around the outside of the hall.' There were various moans and groans, but we started jogging as instructed. She then shouted, 'Right, in a line. Leapfrog next.' I groaned inwardly. I hated this exercise.

The first girl had to get into the leapfrog position, the next would leapfrog over her then join her in the same position. The third had to leapfrog both then stoop to provide yet another back to be jumped. As soon as the last person had taken their turn, it was time for the first girl to jump over everyone, a constantly moving line of leapfrogging girls working a bit like the tracks of a tank.

This resulted in 30 girls one by one pressing down on your back whilst leaping over you. Bearing in mind I was five foot ten, I was taller than most girls so had to bob down a little further in order to give them a fighting chance of clearing me and not kneeing me in the head.

This chain of leapfrogging continued for about ten minutes — a long time and incredibly exhausting. My legs turned to jelly and I felt as if I couldn't go on any longer. Eventually, the PTI blew her whistle and we were told to get into squad. Huffing and puffing, we formed a sorry-looking bunch. She looked over at me and said, 'Stand up straight, McCann.' I looked at her slightly puzzled.

'I *am* standing up straight.'

'No, you are not.' I remained in the same position as I had no idea what she was talking about. She looked irritated and walked over to me whilst the rest of the girls looked on with interest. Tessa, standing in front of me, turned around and started to laugh.

'You look like a boomerang, McCann. She's right, you're standing all drunk,' she chuckled in her heavy Welsh accent. The PTI walked up to me and, placing her arms on either side of my shoulders, tried to straighten me up. A sharp pain ripped through my back and I saw stars. Suddenly, I wobbled and flopped forward slightly into the PTI.

'Shit, get her into the office. Now!' she commanded with some urgency. She looked really worried. 'Get some water,' she ordered one of the girls.

The pain in my back was excruciating and I felt sick. 'Bloody hell, she's as white as a ghost,' I heard Tessa say. 'McCann, girl, the colour's drained from your face, you look see-through.' Any other time, I would have fallen about laughing but, right now, I was scared to move and scared to remain still. The pain was horrendous.

The PTI told everyone to leave the office apart from Dotty and said I'd slipped a disc in my back. I didn't at any point question the fact she wasn't a doctor. She told me to turn over and lie on my stomach. This took about five minutes as the pain was making me sweat, even though I felt frozen to the bone. Eventually, I managed to do as instructed. The PTI told me she needed to put the disc back into place. I had no idea how she was going to do this but, when I felt the heel of her foot connect with the small of my back, I wanted to rip her head off and dropkick it across the gym.

'What the hell are you doing?' I screamed. 'Pack it in! That's not bloody helping!' She was about to bring her heel down again when Dotty screamed at her.

'Stop! Call an ambulance!'

'She doesn't need an ambulance, it isn't life or death.'

Hell, that was easy for her to say. She wasn't the one on the floor, lying on her stomach and dry retching with pain.

'Sod this, I'm driving her to hospital,' Dotty snapped. 'You've probably done more damage, you mental bitch.' Dotty grabbed the phone, called the MT yard, and asked for the duty driver, explaining we needed a car — and fast — to take me to hospital. Within minutes, the car arrived with Mac driving. He took one look at me and exhaled.

'Whhooaahhh, what the hell happened to *her*?'

'No flipping idea, but it ain't good,' Dotty replied. 'Medway Hospital and step on it,' she added. I don't remember the journey to the hospital as I blacked out every time he flew over a bump in the road. I had never felt so much pain in my life.

We got to the hospital and Dotty burst through the A&E doors like Rambo. Looking back, she was really in the moment and I wished I'd been well enough to take off a sock and tie it around her head as a headband.

When it came to the crunch, Dotty was not taking no for an answer. She marched up to the reception desk. 'She needs to see someone right away. She's had an accident and keeps slipping in and out of consciousness.'

The receptionist took one look at me and indicated for a doctor or triage nurse to come and take me to a cubicle with a curtain around it. Dotty helped me onto the gurney which seemed to take forever. I was still randomly dry retching and was sure I was dying.

After around an hour, a doctor came to see me. Dotty briefed him on the situation. He asked me to stand up so he could get a look at my back. Ten minutes later, I'd managed to get into an upright position. He turned me around and asked me to bend over as far as I could manage. I had a flashback to my first night with Sergeant Major Dorset and was sure he had asked me to do something similar.

I felt a moment's panic and then remembered I was in a hospital and the doctor was hardly likely to be doing anything untoward. In any other situation, I would have giggled at the innuendo of the request. I managed to lean forward very slightly and then started to retch again. He muttered to himself a couple of times then said I could get back onto the gurney. As I was taking my time getting back into a lying position, he reached out to help me.

'Don't touch me!' I yelped through gritted teeth. 'Please, just don't touch me. I can do it.' I was terrified of him moving me too quickly and the pain intensifying, assuming that was even possible. The doctor looked very concerned and held his hands up as if to say, 'OK, OK, no problem.'

He disappeared into a sea of people and ten minutes later a nurse appeared with a tray containing a syringe and a bottle of liquid. She addressed Dotty more than me as I was too busy retching. She explained she was going to give me a painkilling injection in my upper thigh. She then gave Dotty instructions that I would need complete bed rest for two weeks. Dotty nodded that she had understood and I willingly took the shot in my leg.

The journey back was easier as the painkiller was now beginning to take effect. We returned to the block and Sergeant Babstock was informed of my situation. She decided it would be better for me to go home for two weeks so I could receive care from my mother.

The following morning, Dotty volunteered to be the driver to take me up to Hull. She was given permission to stay over and return to camp the next day. My mother had been called and had my bed ready for me. My father had placed a large, solid sheet of wood under the mattress to firm it up slightly. I had two weeks' bed rest and, towards the end of the second week, I was up and about a little bit and able to move around.

I still have problems with my back today and have since met up with the PTI who decided to play doctor that day. I gave her a hug as it seemed pointless to drag it all up again after twenty years had passed and I didn't think she needed the worry or the guilt. What was done was done.

44/ Time to go home

After six years of scraping ice off windscreens during the winter months and getting up at five o'clock in the morning for many of my driving details just to spend my days waiting in a vehicle for someone else, I decided to buy myself out of the army. It was March 1987 and I was sure there must be more to life. At the time, I paid £127 which was a lot of money for me back then. It was a huge decision as I knew the outside world would be completely different to the army.

On the day I was due to leave, I told everyone I would see them at lunchtime to say goodbye as my dad was coming to get me. As I got ready, I was nervous he would be late, though I should've known he would never be late for anything, and certainly not when it came to picking me up. I was hopeless at goodbyes so, like a coward, I snuck away at eleven without saying farewell to anyone. I just couldn't face it.

As the years have gone by, I've learned how to deal with the awkwardness of goodbyes and, if I could go back in time, I would have waited to take my leave of everyone. I've remained friends with many of my fantastic army colleagues and have so many memories that still make me smile. Together we had an adventure I'll never forget.

I've never experienced anything like army life. I lived life to the max and enjoyed 99 per cent of every waking moment serving as a British soldier — the one per cent being duties and PT!

As a youngster, I'd been opinionated, spirited, and headstrong, giving my parents grief they didn't need or deserve. I was very selfish and, if I wanted to do something, I did it and bugger the consequences.

The army instilled in me so many good qualities I wouldn't now have, had I not served. It taught me discipline, even though I constantly challenged it. It taught me how to think as part of a team and how my choices could affect others. It taught me how to cope and adapt under pressure and shaped me into a better person. And it taught me respect, not just for my elders like my parents had shown me, but also a deep respect for rank, position, and hierarchy which has seen me in good stead throughout my subsequent careers.

After I left, I was excited as to what the future may hold but, within a few weeks, I worried I'd perhaps made a huge mistake as I felt like a fish out of water. I couldn't sleep in, yet I didn't have anything to get up for. I wandered around with no purpose and struggled to adapt to civilian life.

In the army, life is structured; you do everything at the same time every

147

day whether it be getting up, being on parade, or taking breaks. Each day was planned out for you so, when you decided to leave as I had, with no job to go straight into, it was very hard to spend days without purpose.

The first few months were incredibly difficult and I became lazy and drank a *little* too much with friends for a while. Fortunately, sanity prevailed, though quite why I thought I'd be any good at selling encyclopedias to the American military in Germany is beyond me.

And little did I know what crazy antics my subsequent employment as a chauffeur and bodyguard in the music business would hold but, boy, I was keen to find out.

Appendix - Military ranking

From lowest to highest:

Private	Joining rank
Lance Corporal	One stripe
Corporal	Two stripes
Sergeant	Three stripes
Staff Sergeant	Three stripes with a crown above
Warrant Officer / Sergeant Major	Crown on forearm. 1st Class and 2nd Class
2nd Lieutenant	One pip on epaulettes. Lowest rank of commissioned officer
Lieutenant	Two pips on epaulettes
Captain	Three pips on epaulettes
Major	Crown on epaulettes
Lieutenant Colonel	One pip and a crown on epaulettes
Colonel	Two pips and a crown on epaulettes
Brigadier	Three pips and a crown on epaulettes
Major General	Cross swords and a pip on epaulettes
Lieutenant General	Cross swords and a crown on epaulettes
General	Cross swords, a pip, and a crown on epaulettes
Field Marshall	Two crossed batons surrounded by a yellow leaf below St Edward's Crown on epaulettes

Acknowledgements

I owe a huge debt of gratitude to many people who have been there for me, through thick and thin. Sincere thanks to the following:

My sister, brother-in-law, and nieces for your constant support, for believing in me, and for not judging my sometimes outrageous choices and decisions. I love you immensely.

My school teachers, who did the best they could with the material they had. I owe you an apology for sure.

My superiors in the army who, with great difficulty, helped shape me into the person I am today. I probably didn't seem very grateful at the time.

My best friend, Linda, who frequently reminds me that shit just happens to me and I should be grateful for her loyalty.

Nic, for encouraging me to finish this book and for all her advice.

Sam, whom I share an office with. Despite my wittering on about this book incessantly, she gallantly stepped in to help me with the final bits.

Ant Press, my publishers, for their belief, advice, support, and for producing the finished product.

Graham D. Lock, illustrator and designer, for the fantastic job he made of turning some of my funny stories into visuals for the cover.

It is impossible to mention everyone who has influenced my life in one way or another but you know who you are. Whether your input was negative or positive, I learned from it and I thank you for it.

It's been a blast to date.

Contact the author

I sincerely thank you for reading this book and hope you enjoyed it. I would be extremely grateful if you could leave a review on Amazon.

I'd also love to hear your comments and am happy to answer any questions you may have, so do please get in touch with me by:

- Email: lornamccann64@gmail.com

If you would like to be notified when my next book is published, please do send me an email now.

If you enjoy memoirs, I recommend you pop over to Facebook group We Love Memoirs to chat with me and other authors there. www.facebook.com/groups/welovememoirs

I look forward to hearing from you.

Lorna McCann

Ant Press books

If you enjoyed this book, you may also enjoy these titles:

Chickens, Mules and Two Old Fools by Victoria Twead
(Wall Street Journal Top 10 bestseller)

Two Old Fools ~ Olé! by Victoria Twead

Two Old Fools on a Camel by Victoria Twead
(New York Times bestseller x 3)

Two Old Fools in Spain Again by Victoria Twead

One Young Fool in Dorset by Victoria Twead

Simon Ships Out: How one brave, stray cat became a worldwide hero by Jacky Donovan

Instant Whips and Dream Toppings: A true-life dom rom com by Jacky Donovan

Heartprints of Africa: A Family's Story of Faith, Love, Adventure, and Turmoil: Volume 1 by Cinda Adams Brooks

Into Africa with 3 Kids, 13 Crates and a Husband by Ann Patras

Paw Prints in Oman: Dogs, Mogs and Me by Charlotte Smith
(New York Times bestseller)

Joan's Descent into Alzheimer's by Jill Stoking

The Girl Behind the Painted Smile: My battle with the bottle by Catherine Lockwood

The Coconut Chronicles: Two Guys, One Caribbean Dream House by Patrick Youngblood

Fat Dogs and French Estates ~ Part I by Beth Haslam
Fat Dogs and French Estates ~ Part II by Beth Haslam

Midwife: A Calling (Memoirs of an Urban Midwife Book I) by Peggy Vincent

Printed in Great Britain
by Amazon.co.uk, Ltd.,
Marston Gate.